Country Hits

Published by
Wise Publications
14-15 Berners Street,
London W1T 3LJ, UK.

Exclusive Distributors:
Music Sales Limited
Distribution Centre,
Newmarket Road, Bury St Edmunds,
Suffolk IP33 3YB, UK.
Music Sales Pty Limited
20 Resolution Drive, Caringbah,
NSW 2229, Australia.

Order No. AM997502
ISBN 978-1-84938-092-8

Compiled by Nick Crispin.
Text by Graham Vickers.
Picture research by Jacqui Black.
Music engraved by Paul Ewers Music Design.
Edited by Tom Farncombe and Adrian Hopkins.
Design by Fresh Lemon.

www.musicsales.com

Printed in China.

Photograph credits:

Page 5:
Waylon Jennings performs at Alex
Cooley's Capri Ballroom on February 17,
1979 in Atlanta, Georgia. (Photo by Tom
Hill/GettyImages)

Page 7:
Carter family (Getty Images)

Page 18:
Hank Williams
(Michael Ochs Archives/Getty Images)

Page 38:
Ray Price - 1950s
(Everett Collection/Rex Features)

Page 39:
Patsy Cline (LFI)

Page 77:
Johnny Cash (LFI)

Page 96:
Willie Nelson (LFI)

Page 144:
Kris Kristofferson (LFI)

Page 155:
Tammy Wynette (LFI)

Page 180:
'Hee Haw' TV Series - 1969 -
Kenny Rogers
(NBCUPHOTOBANK/Rex Features)

Page 181:
George Jones (LFI)

Page 206:
Dolly Parton (LFI)

Page 230:
Steve Earle (LFI)

Page 240:
Alison Krauss performing at
the New Orleans Jazz Festival,
New Orleans, America -
25 Apr 2008 (Sipa Press/Rex Features)

Page 250:
Vince Gill (LFI)

Page 251:
Dixie Chicks (LFI)

Page 272:
Garth Brooks, Las Vegas, America,
13 August 1998 (Rex Features)

Wise Publications
part of The Music Sales Group
London / New York / Paris / Sydney / Copenhagen / Berlin / Tokyo / Madrid

Introduction

This terrific collection of Country songs reflects the wide musical variety to be found within a genre sometimes criticised for "all sounding the same".

Absolutely no one sounded like Hank Williams whose 'Your Cheatin' Heart', 'I Saw The Light' and 'Jambalaya' are featured here alongside many others. Williams sang a straight-ahead brand of country during his short, troubled career—no frills, just heartfelt lyrics that left you in no doubt that life and love could be hard in the rural communities of the American south after the Depression. By contrast his contemporary Lefty Frizzell ('Long Black Veil') specialised in intricate vocal phrasing that would be a heavy influence on future country singers, most notably George Jones, Merle Haggard, Keith Whitley and Alan Jackson.

After a long and successful career as a honky-tonk singer George Jones turned to ballads and in 1980 had one of his biggest hits with 'He Stopped Loving Her Today', frequently nominated as the greatest country song of all time. A superb stylist whom the rarely-modest Frank Sinatra once called 'the second-best singer in America', Jones somehow managed to survive a life of frightening alcohol and drug abuse and continues recording and performing well into his seventies.

Charlie Rich ('The Most Beautiful Girl') who had been stable mate to Elvis Presley at Sun Records brought a touch of smooth blues to country music and songwriter Willie Nelson introduced understated wit and classy melodies to the genre ('Hello Walls', 'Crazy', 'Funny How Time Slips Away').

Rhinestone glitz came from Dolly Parton ('I Will Always Love You', 'Jolene', 'Coat of Many Colours') and she shone so brightly that she was a star before anyone realised that beneath the low-rent floozy disguise she was an exquisite singer, a great songwriter, smart as a whip and even better than Madonna at image management.

Over the years country has kept crossing over to the mainstream and back again. Guy Mitchell ('Singing The Blues'), Olivia Newton-John ('Take Me Home, Country Roads') and Marie Osmond ('Paper Roses') were hardly country singers but they all had country hits in the pop charts. Steve Earle ('Copperhead Road') and Waylon Jennings ('I've Always Been Crazy'), pictured right, couldn't have gone mainstream to save their lives, while intelligent, un-showbizzy women like Alison Krauss and Mary Chapin Carpenter just let the songs speak for themselves and resisted the lure of big hair and sequins. Carpenter's 'He Thinks He'll Keep Her' remains a searing feminist broadside at the 'Stand By Your Man' mentality.

This GigBook compilation reflects something of all that variety and a lot more. Choose your favourites and start playing and singing. They won't all sound the same, we promise!

OVER **100** CLASSIC SONGS

Many early country hits were folk songs

that often became identified with particular performers. 'Cripple Creek' was a mountain banjo tune that became a favourite in the repertoire of many bluegrass bands including that of Bill Monroe. 'The Yellow Rose of Texas' was a traditional song that became associated with singing cowboy Gene Autry and achieved pop fame in the 1950s after it was used in the James Dean movie Giant, and Mitch Miller's recording was brilliantly parodied by Stan Freberg. 'Home On The Range', the state song of Kansas, was based on a romantic, patriotic poem and has become a classic.

'Wabash Cannonball' was one of the first of many country paeans to trains, in this case a mythical one. The Carter Family recorded it first in 1929 but it became more closely associated with Roy Acuff after his 1936 version was released. 'The Orange Blossom Special' was another train song, one that became a classic virtuoso piece for fiddlers (and other instrumentalists) down the years.

The Carter Family

Cripple Creek

Traditional

Bright country style

1. Just put on a brand new suit, hair - cut, shave and shine to boot,

(Verse 2 see block lyrics)

dia - mond stick - pin in my tie, see you lat - er folks, good - bye!

Go - ing to Crip - ple Creek, not for swim - min', go - ing to Crip - ple Creek, here's why,

down by Crip - ple Creek a - mong some wo - men I met the ap - ple of my eye!

Verse 2:
Man! That gal has me bewitched
All dressed up for gettin' hitched!
Gonna meet her, cheek to cheek
In the church by Cripple Creek
Going to Cripple Creek.

The Lonesome Road

Words by Gene Austin
Music by Nathaniel Shilkret

Moderately

Look down, look down, that lone - some road,___ be - -fore you tra - vel on.___ Look up, look up, and see yo' Mak - er, 'fore Ga - briel blows his horn.___ Wea - ry to - tin' such a load, tredg - in' down that lone - some road. Look down, look down, that lone - some road,___ be - fore you tra - vel on.___ Look ___

The Yellow Rose Of Texas

Traditional

Moderately

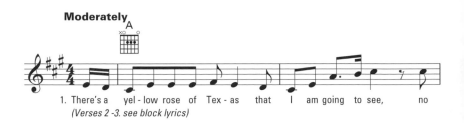

1. There's a yel - low rose of Tex - as that I am going to see, no
(Verses 2 -3. see block lyrics)

oth - er fel - low knows her, no oth - er, on - ly me. she

cried so when I left her, it al - most broke my heart, and

if I ev - er find her, we nev - er more will part. She's the

sweet - est rose of Tex - as this fel - low ev - er knew, her

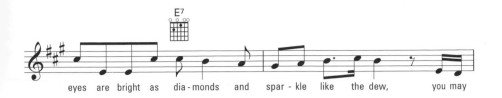

eyes are bright as dia-monds and spar-kle like the dew, you may

talk a-bout your dear-est maids and sing of Ros-a-lie, but the

yel-low rose of Tex-as beats the belles of Ten-nes-see.

Verse 2:
Where the Rio Grande is flowing and stars are shining bright
We walked along the river one quiet summer night
She said, "If you remember, we parted long ago
You promised to come back to me and never leave me so."

Verse 3:
So I'm going back to meet her because I love her so
We'll sing the songs together that we sang so long ago
I'll play the banjo gaily and we'll sing the songs of yore
And the yellow rose of Texas shall be mine forever more.

Home On The Range

Words by Brewster Higley
Music by Daniel Kelley

Moderately

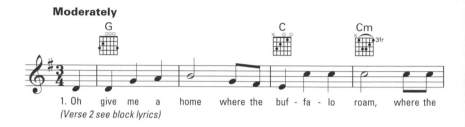

1. Oh give me a home where the buf - fa - lo roam, where the
(Verse 2 see block lyrics)

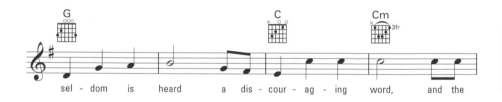

deer and the an - te - lope play._____ Where

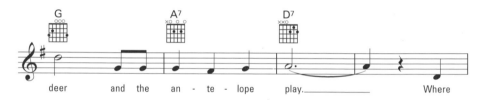

sel - dom is heard a dis - cour - ag - ing word, and the

skies are not cloud - y all day._____

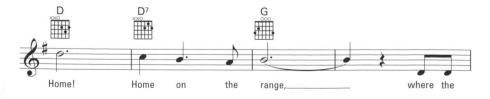

Home! Home on the range,_____ where the

12

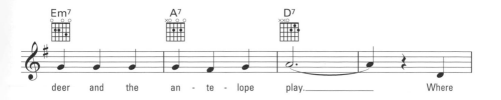

deer and the an - te - lope play._____ Where

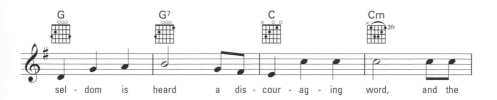

sel - dom is heard a dis - cour - ag - ing word, and the

skies are not cloud - y all day._____

Verse 2:
How often at night when the heavens are bright
With the light from the glittering stars
Have I stood there amazed and asked as I gazed
If their glory exceeds that of ours.

Wabash Cannon Ball

Words & Music by A. P. Carter

Moderately

1. From out the wide Pa - ci - fic to the broad At - lan - tic

(Verses 2-5. see block lyrics)

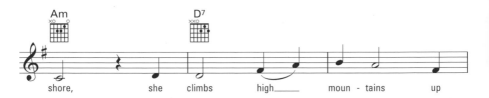

shore, she climbs high_____ moun - tains up

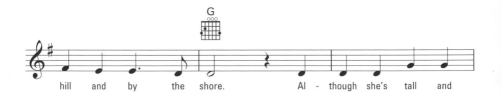

hill and by the shore. Al - though she's tall and

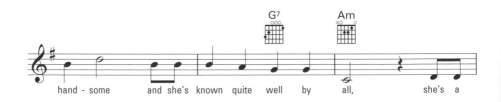

hand - some and she's known quite well by all, she's a

reg - 'lar com - bi - na - tion of the Wa - bash Can - non -

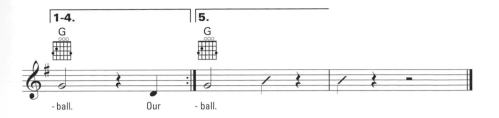

Verse 2:
Our eastern states are dandies, so the western people say
When she climbed old Rock Island took all her style away
To the Lakes of Minnesota where the ripling waters fall
No changes can be taken on the Wabash Cannon Ball.

Verse 3:
She came down from Birmingham one cold December day
As she pulled in to the station, you could hear all the people say
"There's the gal from Tennessee; she is long and she is tall
She comes from Birmingham on the Wabash Cannon Ball."

Verse 4:
Just listen to the jingle and the rumble and the roar
As she glides along the woodland to the hills and by the shore
Hear the mighty rush of the engine, hear the lonesome hobos call
While she's trav'lling through the jungle on the Wabash Cannon Ball.

Verse 5:
Here's to old man daddy Claxton, may his name forever stand
May it always be remembered throughout the land
His earthly race is over, and the curtains 'round him fall
We'll carry him home to vict'ry on the Wabash Cannon Ball.

The Orange Blossom Special

Words & Music by Ervin T. Rouse

Verse 2:
I'm goin' down to Flor'da and get some sand in my shoes
Or maybe California and get some sand in my shoes
I'll ride that Orange blossom special
And lose these New York blues.

Verse 3:
Talk about a-trav'lin', she's the fastest train on the line
Talk about a-trav'lin', she's the fastest train on the line
It's that Orange blossom special
Rollin' down the Seaboard line.

The forties were a golden period in country music

The legendary Hank Williams (above) was enjoying his all-too-brief heyday (he would be dead at 29 by late 1953). Bill Monroe recorded a sedate waltz version of 'Blue Moon of Kentucky' (years later he would speed it up to echo Elvis Presley's cover version) and Roy Acuff's 1945 recording of 'Blue Eyes Crying In The Rain' first popularised a song that Willie Nelson would make into a huge hit in 1975 when it was featured on his 'Red Headed Stranger' album.

Born To Lose

Words & Music by Ted Daffan

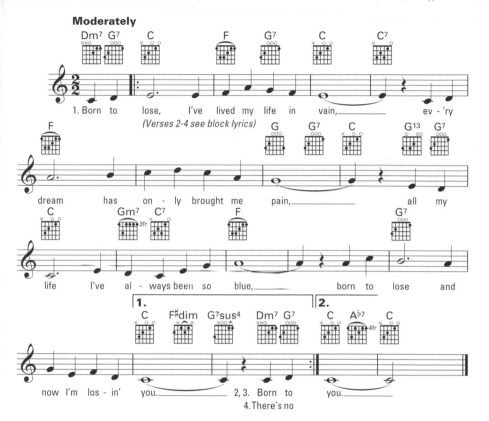

1. Born to lose, I've lived my life in vain,_____ ev - 'ry
(Verses 2-4 see block lyrics)

dream has on - ly brought me pain,_____ all my

life I've al - ways been so blue,_____ born to lose and

now I'm los - in' you._____ 2, 3. Born to you.
4. There's no

Verse 2:
Born to lose, it seems so hard to bear
How I long to always have you near
You've grown tired and now you say we're through
Born to lose and now I'm losin' you.

Verse 3:
Born to lose, my every hope is gone
It's so hard to face that empty dawn
You were all the happiness I knew
Born to lose and now I'm losin' you.

Verse 4:
There's no use to dream of happiness
All I see is only loneliness
All my life I've always been so blue
Born to lose and now I'm losin' you.

19

Deep In The Heart Of Texas

Words by June Hershey
Music by Don Swander

Moderately bright

1. There is a land, a west-ern land, might-y won-der-ful to see.____ It is the land I un-der-stand, and it's there I long to be.____ 2. The stars at night are big and bright,

(Verse 3 see block lyrics)

(clap)

deep in the heart of Tex-as; the

Verse 3:
The coyotes wail along the trail
Deep in the heart of Texas
The rabbits rush around the brush
Deep in the heart of Texas
The cowboys cry, "Kiyippeevi"
Deep in the heart of Texas
The dogies bawl, and bawl and bawl
Deep in the heart of Texas.

Blue Eyes Crying In The Rain

Words & Music by Fred Rose

Moderately

1. In the twi - light glow I see her,_____
(Verse 2 see block lyrics)

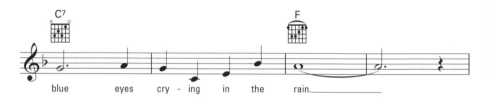

blue eyes cry - ing in the rain._____

As we kissed good - bye and part - ed, I

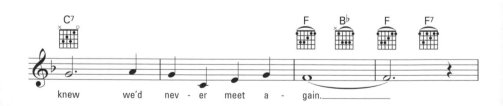

knew we'd nev - er meet a - gain._____

Love is like a dy - ing em - ber,_____

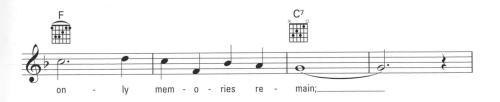

on - ly mem - o - ries re - main;_____

through the a - ges I'll re - mem - ber,_____

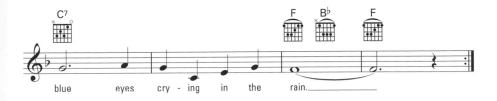

blue eyes cry - ing in the rain._____

Verse 2:
Now my hair has turned to silver
All my life I've loved in vain
I can see her star in heaven
Blue eyes crying in the rain
Someday when we meet up yonder
We'll stroll hand in hand again
In a land that knows no parting
Blue eyes crying in the rain.

Blue Moon Of Kentucky

Words & Music by Bill Monroe

Bright 'jump' tempo

Blue moon,_____ blue moon,_____ blue

moon_____ keep a - shin - in' bright,_____ blue

moon, keep__ on a - shin - in' bright,__ you're gon - na bring-a me back - a my

ba - by to night.__ Blue moon, keep a-shin - in' bright!_____ I said blue

moon of Ken - tuck - y, to keep on shin - ing,_____ shine

on the one that's gone and left me blue,___ I said blue

24

moon of Ken-tuck-y to keep on shin - ing,_____ shine

on the one that's gone and left__ me blue.__ Well it was

on one moon-light night, stars shin-in' bright.

Whis - per on high, love_____ said good-bye, blue

moon of Ken-tuck-y, keep on shin - ing,_____ shine

1.
on the one that's gone and left__ me blue.__

2.
I said blue _____

Sixteen Tons

Words & Music by Merle Travis

Moderately

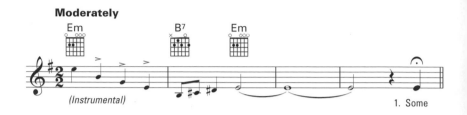

(Instrumental)

1. Some

peo-ple say a man is made out of mud,— a poor man's made out of
(Verses 2 -4. see block lyrics)

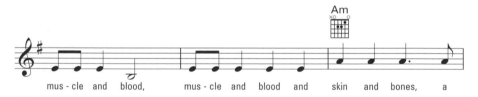

mus-cle and blood, mus-cle and blood and skin and bones, a

mind that's_ weak and a back that's strong. You load six-teen tons,

what do you get?_ An-oth-er day old-er and deep-er in debt._ Say

broth - er don't you call me, 'cause I can't go,___ I

owe___ my soul to the com - pa - ny store.___

2. I was ___

Verse 2:
I was born one mornin' when the sun didn't shine
I picked up my shovel and I walked to the mine
I loaded sixteen tons of number nine coal
And the straw boss said "Well, bless my soul".

Verse 3:
I was born one mornin', it was drizzlin' rain
Fightin' and trouble are my middle name
I was raised in the canebrake by an ole mama lion
Cain't no high-toned woman make me walk the line.

Verse 4:
If you see me comin', better step aside
A lotta men didn't, a lotta men died
One fist of iron, the other of steel
If the right one don't get you then the left one will.

27

I Saw The Light

Words & Music by Hank Williams

Brightly

1. I wan - dered so aim - less, life filled with

(Verses 2 & 3 see block lyrics)

sin, I would - n't let my dear Sav - iour

in.____ Then Je - sus came like a

strang - er in the night, praise the Lord____

I saw the light. I saw the light____

I saw the light,____ no more dark - ness,

no more   night.____   Now I'm   so   hap - py,   no

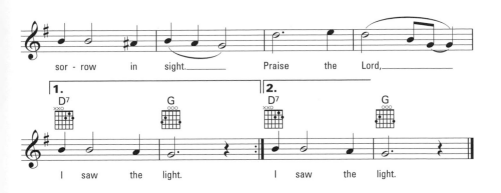

sor - row   in   sight.____   Praise   the   Lord,____

1. | **2.**

I   saw   the   light.   I   saw   the   light.

Verse 2:
Just like a blind man I wandered along
Worries and fears I claimed for my own
Then like the blind man that God gave back his sight
Praise the Lord, praise the Lord I saw the light.

Verse 3:
I was a fool to wander and stray
Straight is the gate and narrow the way
Now I have traded the wrong for the right
Praise the Lord, praise the Lord I saw the light.

A Mansion On The Hill

Words by Fred Rose
Music by Hank Williams

Moderately

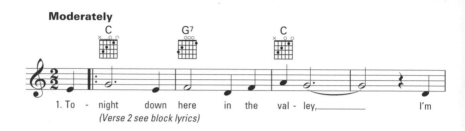

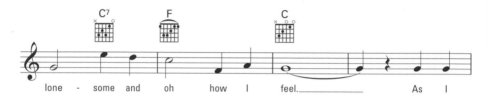

1. To - night down here in the val - ley,_____ I'm
(Verse 2 see block lyrics)

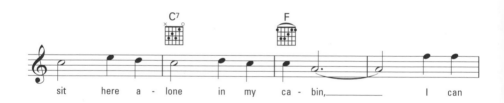

lone - some and oh how I feel._____ As I

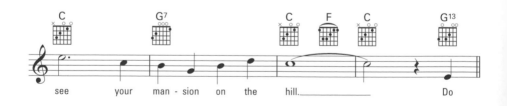

sit here a - lone in my ca - bin,_____ I can

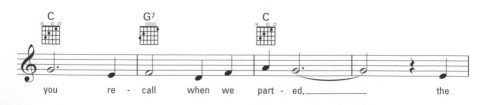

see your man - sion on the hill._____ Do

you re - call when we part - ed,_____ the

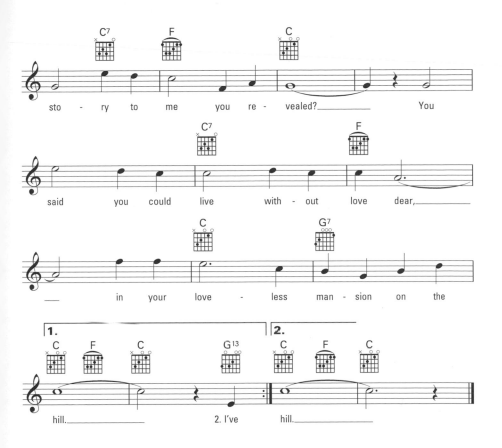

sto - ry to me you re - vealed?_____ You
said you could live with - out love dear,_____
____ in your love - less man - sion on the

1.
hill._____ 2. I've

2.
hill._____

Verse 2:
I've waited all through the years love
To give you a heart true and real
'Cause I know you're living in sorrow
In your loveless mansion on the hill

The light shines bright from your window
The trees stand so silent and still
I know you're alone with your pride dear
In your loveless mansion on the hill.

Tennessee Waltz

Words & Music by Redd Stewart & Pee Wee King

Moderately

I was waltz - ing____ with my darl - in'____ to the

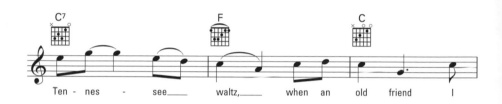

Ten - nes - see____ waltz,____ when an old friend I

hap - pened to see.____ In - tro - duced him____ to my

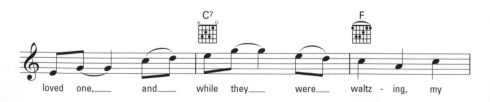

loved one,____ and____ while they____ were____ waltz - ing, my

friend stole my sweet-heart from me._____ I re-
-mem-ber the night and the Ten-nes-see waltz, now I
know just how much I have lost._____
_____ Yes I lost my_____ lit-tle darl-in'_____ the_____
night they_____ were_____ play-ing, the beau-ti-ful Ten-nes-see

1.
waltz._____ I was

2.
waltz._____

My Son Calls Another Man Daddy

Words by Jewell House
Music by Hank Williams

Expressively

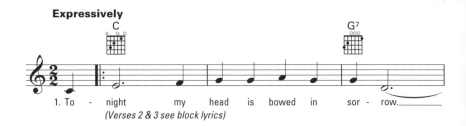

1. To - night my head is bowed in sor - row.

(Verses 2 & 3 see block lyrics)

I can't keep the tears from my eyes.

My son calls an - oth - er man dad - dy.

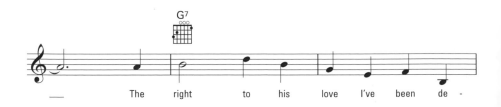

The right to his love I've been de -

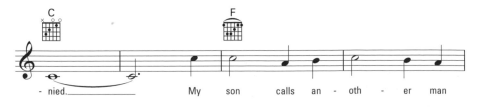

- nied. My son calls an - oth - er man

34

dad - dy,_____ he'll ne'er know my name or my

face._____ God on - ly knows how it

hurts me_____ for an - oth - er to be in my

1, 2. | **3.**

place._____ 2, 3. Each place._____

Verse 2:
Each night I laid there in prison
I pictured a future so bright
And he was the one ray of sunshine
That shone through the darkness of night.

Verse 3:
Each day his mother shares a new love
She just couldn't stand my disgrace
My son calls another man daddy
And longs for a love he can't replace.

I'm So Lonesome I Could Cry

Words & Music by Hank Williams

Moderately

1. Hear_____ that lone - some whip - poor - will? He
(Verse 2 see block lyrics)

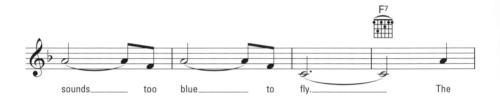

sounds_____ too blue_____ to fly._____ The

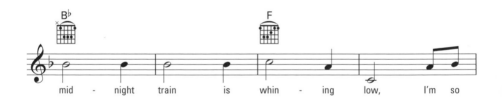

mid - night train is whin - ing low, I'm so

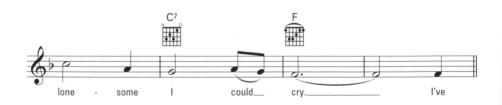

lone - some I could___ cry._____ I've

nev - er seen_____ a night_____ so

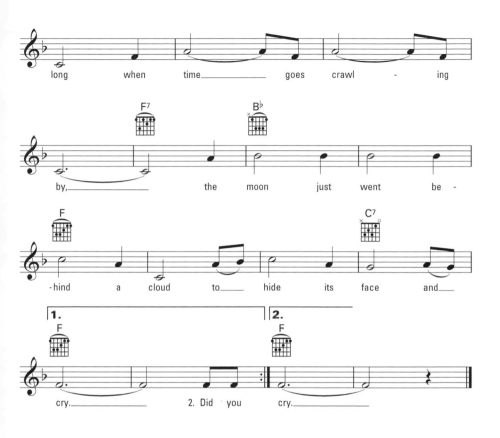

long   when   time_____   goes   crawl -   ing

by,_____   the   moon   just   went   be -

-hind   a   cloud   to____ hide   its   face   and____

1. cry._____   2. Did you   **2.** cry._____

Verse 2:
Did you ever see a robin weep
When leaves began to die?
That means he's lost the will to live
I'm so lonesome I could cry.
The silence of a falling star
Lights up a purple sky
And as I wonder where you are
I'm so lonesome I could cry.

This was the decade when country first went metropolitan

Hank Williams songs lent themselves to blander cover versions by Tony Bennett ('Cold Cold Heart') and Jo Stafford & Frankie Laine ('Hey Good Lookin'). Meanwhile Slim Willet's off-the-beat 'Don't Let The Stars Get in Your Eyes' received a makeover from the ever-relaxed—sometimes seemingly comatose—Perry Como. Melvyn Endsley's 'Singing The Blues' never had a true country recording but Guy Mitchell, Marty Robbins and Tommy Steele all had versions that added various shades of country. Western theme tunes became popular with Frankie Laine's dramatic voice usually favourite to take on the latest stirring Hollywood song about gunfights or cattle drives. Lefty Frizzell, Hank Williams' only real jukebox rival in the American south, never enjoyed the same degree of wider popularity but the death-ditty 'Long Black Veil' was a notable 1959 hit for him. Also in 1959, Jim Reeves, who would become one of country music's all-time biggest sellers, arrived in the charts with 'He'll Have To Go', a pop-flavoured country song that would become a classic and was recorded by both Elvis Presley and Ry Cooder. Other hits included 'Crazy Arms' by Ray Price (above) and Patsy Cline's 'Sweet Dreams'.

Patsy Cline

Cold, Cold Heart

Words & Music by Hank Williams

40

things I did - n't do. In an - ger, un - kind words are said that

make the tear - drops start. Why can't I free your doubt - ful mind and

1. melt your cold, cold heart? 2. You'll **2.** melt your cold, cold heart?

Verse 2:
You'll never know how much it hurts to see you sit and cry
You know you need and want my love, yet you're afraid to try
Why do you run and hide from life? To try it just ain't smart
Why can't I free your doubtful mind and melt your cold, cold heart?

There was a time when I believed that you belong to me
But now I know your heart is shackled to a memory
The more I learn to care for you, the more we drift apart
Why can't I free your doubtful mind and melt your cold, cold heart?

Hey, Good Lookin'

Words & Music by Hank Williams

Moderately

1. Hey, hey, good look-in', what-cha got cook-in',
(Verse 2 see block lyrics)

how's a-bout cook-in' some-thin' up____ with me.____

Hey, sweet ba-by, don't____ you think may-be,

we could find us a brand new re - ci - pe.____

—— I got a hot rod Ford and a two dol-lar bill and

I know a spot right ov-er the hill.____ There's so-da pop and the

danc-in's free.___ So if you wan-na have fun come a-long with me.___

Hey, good look-in', what - cha got

cook-in'. How's a-bout cook-in' some-thin' up___ with

1. me.___ 2. I'm

2. me.___

Verse 2:
I'm free and ready so we can go steady
How's about savin' all your time for me
No more lookin', I know I've been tooken
How's about keepin' steady company
I'm gonna throw my date book over the fence
And find me one for five or ten cents
I'll keep it 'til it's covered with age
'Cause I'm writin' your name on every page
Hey, good lookin', whatcha got cookin'
How's about cookin' somethin' up with me.

Jambalaya (On The Bayou)

Words & Music by Hank Williams

1. Good-bye Joe, me got-ta go, me oh my oh,_____ me got-ta

(Verses 2 & 3 see block lyrics)

go pole the pi - rogue down the bay - ou._____ My Y -

- vonne, the sweet - est one, me oh my oh,_____ Son of a

gun, we'll have big fun on the bay - ou._____ Jam - ba -

- la - ya and a craw fish pie and fil - let gum - bo_____

_____ 'cause to - night I'm gon - na see my ma cher a -

1, 2.

3.

-mi - o._____ Pick gui - tar, fill fruit jar and be
gay - o,_____ son of a gun, we'll have big fun on the
bay - ou._____ 2. Thi - bo bay - ou._____

Verse 2:
Thibo daux Fontain aux, the place is buzzin'
Kinfolk come to see Yvonne by the dozen
Dress in style and go hog wild, me oh my oh
Son of a gun, we'll have big fun on the bayou.

Verse 3:
Settle down far from town, get me a pirogue
And I'll catch all the fish in the bayou
Swap my mon to buy Yvonne what she need-o
Son of a gun, we'll have big fun on the bayou.

How's The World Treating You

Words & Music by Chet Atkins & Boudleaux Bryant

Moderately slow

Capo fret 1

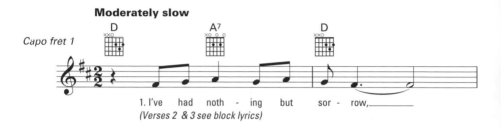

1. I've had noth - ing but sor - row,_____
(Verses 2 & 3 see block lyrics)

since you said we were through, there's no hope for to -

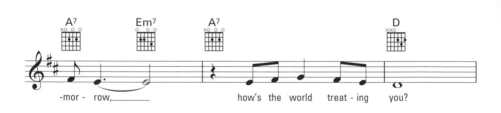

-mor - row,_____ how's the world treat - ing you?

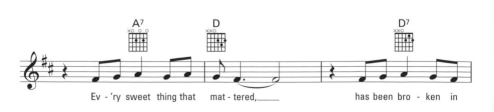

Ev - 'ry sweet thing that mat - tered,_____ has been bro - ken in

two,   all my dreams have been   shat - tered,

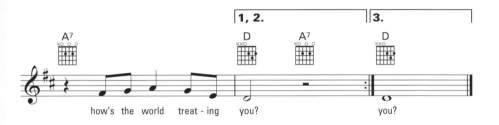

how's the world   treat - ing   you?   you?

Verse 2:
Got no plans for next Sunday
Got no plans for today
Ev'ry day is blue Monday
Ev'ry day you're away

Though our pathways have parted
To your mem'ry I'm true
Guess I'll stay broken hearted
How's the world treating you?

Verse 3:
Do you wonder about me
Like I'm hoping you do?
Are you lonesome without me?
Have you found someone new?

Are you burning and yearning
Do you ever get blue?
Do you think of returning?
How's the world treating you?

Take These Chains From My Heart

Words & Music by Hy Heath & Fred Rose

1. Take these chains from my heart and set me free,_____ you've grown
(Verse 2 see block lyrics)

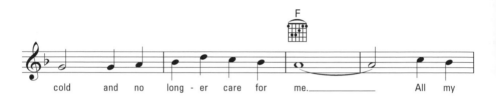

cold and no long-er care for me._____ All my

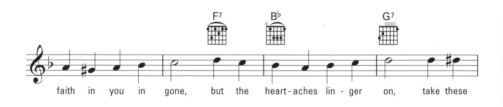

faith in you in gone, but the heart-aches lin-ger on, take these

chains from my heart and set me free._____ Take these

tears from my eyes and let me see,_____ just a

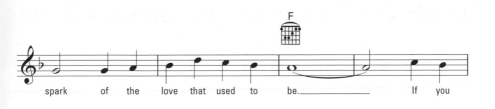

spark of the love that used to be._____ If you

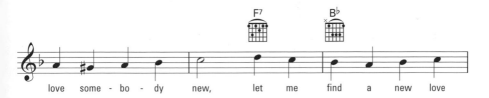

love some - bo - dy new, let me find a new love

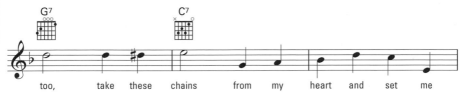

too, take these chains from my heart and set me

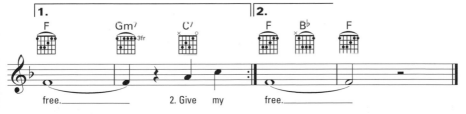

1. free._____ 2. Give my **2.** free._____

Verse 2:
Give my heart just a word of sympathy
Be as fair to my heart as you can be
Then if you no longer care for the love
That's beating there
Take these chains from my heart and set me free.

Take these chains from my heart
And set me free
You've grown cold and no longer care for me
All my faith in you is gone
But the heartaches linger on
Take these chains from my heart and set me free.

Don't Let The Stars Get In Your Eyes

Words & Music by Slim Willet

Brightly

Don't let the stars get in your eyes, don't let the moon break your

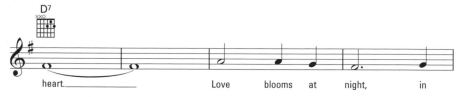

heart._____ Love blooms at night, in

day - light it dies, don't let the stars get in your eyes. Oh keep your

heart for me, for some day I'll re - turn and you know you're the on - ly

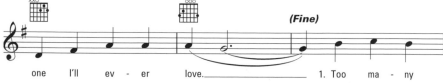

(Fine)

one I'll ev - er love._____ 1. Too ma - ny

nights,_____ too ma - ny stars,_____

(Verse 2 see block lyrics)

50

too ma-ny moons could change your mind._____ If

I'm gone too long, don't for-get where you be-

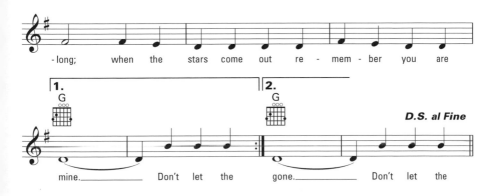

-long; when the stars come out re-mem-ber you are

1.
G

mine._____ Don't let the

2.
G

D.S. al Fine

gone._____ Don't let the

Verse 2:
Too many miles, too many days
Too many nights to be alone
Oh, please keep your heart while we're apart
Don't linger in the moonlight while I'm gone.

Your Cheatin' Heart

Words & Music by Hank Williams

Moderately

1. Your cheat - in' heart will make you weep,
(Verse 2 see block lyrics)

1. you'll cry and cry and try to sleep.

2. But sleep won't will tell on you. When tears come

down like fall - in' rain, you'll toss a - round and call my

name. You'll walk the floor the way I do.

Your cheat - in' heart will tell on you.

Verse 2:
But sleep won't come the whole night through
Your cheatin' heart will tell on you.

I Walk The Line

Words & Music by Johnny Cash

Moderately bright

1. I keep a close watch on this heart of mine._____ I keep my

(Verses 2-5. see block lyrics)

eyes wide op-en all the time._____ I keep the

ends out for the tie that binds._____ Be-cause you're

mine,_____ I walk the line._____ 2. I find it _____

Verse 2:
I find it very, very easy to be true
I find myself alone when each day is through
Yes, I'll admit I'm a fool for you
Because you're mine, I walk the line.

Verse 3:
As sure as night is dark and day is light
I keep you on my mind both day and night
And happiness I've known proves that it's right
Because you're mine, I walk the line.

Verse 4:
You've got a way to keep me on your side
You give me cause for love that I can't hide
For you I know I'd even try to turn the tide
Because you're mine, I walk the line.

Verse 5:
I keep a close watch on this heart of mine
I keep my eyes wide open all the time
I keep the ends out for the tie that binds
Because you're mine, I walk the line.

Singing The Blues

Words & Music by Melvin Endsley

Moderately

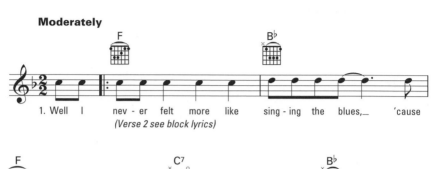

1. Well I nev - er felt more like sing - ing the blues,___ 'cause

(Verse 2 see block lyrics)

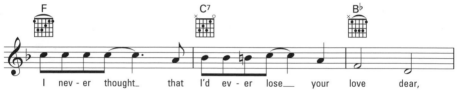

I nev - er thought___ that I'd ev - er lose___ your love dear,

1.

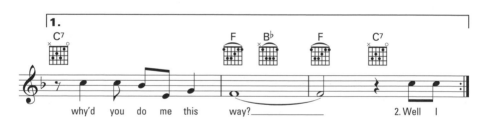

why'd you do me this way?_____ 2. Well I

2.

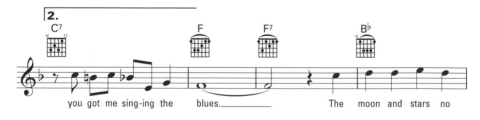

you got me sing-ing the blues._____ The moon and stars no

long - er shine, the dream is gone I thought was mine, there's

no - thing left for me to do but cry____

ov - er you.__ Well, I nev - er felt more like run - ning a - way,__ But

why should I go,__ 'cause I could - n't stay__ with - out you,

you got me sing - ing the blues.__

Verse 2:
Well I never felt more like cryin' all night
'Cause everything's wrong
And nothin' ain't right without you
You got me singing the blues.

Sweet Dreams

Words & Music by Don Gibson

1. Sweet_____ dreams of you,_____ ev - 'ry

(Verse 2 see block lyrics)

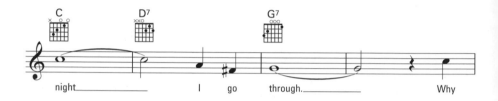

night_____ I go through._____ Why

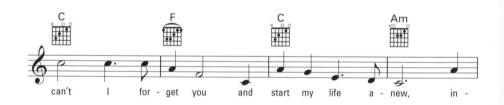

can't I for - get you and start my life a - new, in -

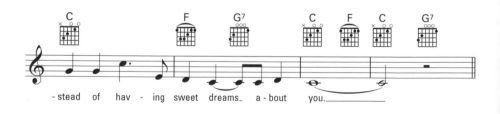

- stead of hav - ing sweet dreams_ a - bout you.

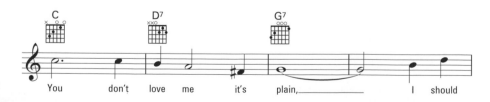

You don't love me it's plain,_____ I should

56

Verse 2:
Sweet dreams of you
Things I know can't come true
Why can't I forget the past,
Start loving someone new
Instead of having sweet dreams about you.

The 3:10 To Yuma

Words by Ned Washington
Music by George W. Duning

Moderately slow

I want to ride a-gain on the three ten to Yu-ma, that's where I saw my love, the girl with the gold-en hair, not a word be-tween us was spo-ken, no the si-lence nev-er was bro-ken, but be-fore she left her eyes said a sad good-bye. Sad am I, sad am I, to think of the chance that I missed, I could cry to

think of the lips left un - kissed._____ Per - haps she'll ride a - gain_____

___ on the three ten to Yu - ma,_____ and I can meet my love and

tell her how much I care,_____ though I have no rea - son to

go there, and there's not a soul that I know there, when the three ten to Yu - ma

leaves if I have the fare,_____ I'll be there!_____

___ I'll be there!_____

Crazy Arms

Words & Music by Chuck Seals & Ralph Mooney

Moderately

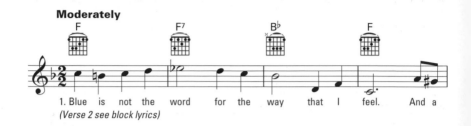

1. Blue is not the word for the way that I feel. And a
(Verse 2 see block lyrics)

storm is brew-ing in this heart of mine.____

This ain't no cra-zy dream, I know that it's real. You're

some-one else -'s love now you're not mine.____

Cra - zy arms that reach to hold some-bo-dy

60

Verse 2:
Please take the treasured dreams
I've had for you and me
And take all the love I thought was mine
Someday my crazy arms my hold someone new
But now I'm so lonely all the time.

Wagon Train

Words & Music by Henri Rene & Bob Russell

Easy country style

Capo fret 1

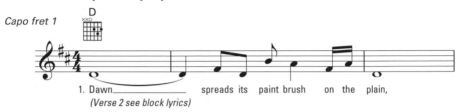

1. Dawn_____ spreads its paint brush on the plain,
(Verse 2 see block lyrics)

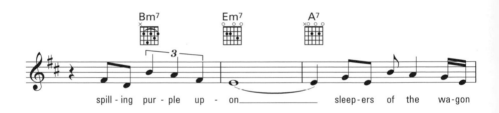

spill - ing pur - ple up - on_____ sleep - ers of the wa - gon

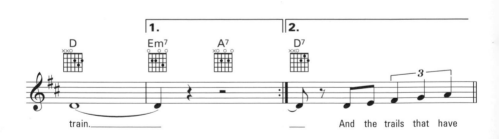

train._____ ___ And the trails that have

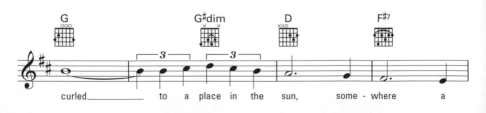

curled_____ to a place in the sun, some - where a

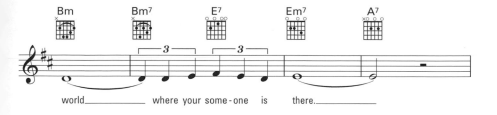

world_____ where your some-one is there._____

Gone_____ are the days of that ter - rain, yet I'm wan-der-ing

on_____ like the old old wa-gon train._____

Verse 2:
Dreams weren't always dreamed in vain
Though the dawn of their schemes
Lay beyond the wagon train.

Oh, Lonesome Me

Words & Music by Don Gibson

Moderately

1. Ev-'ry-bo-dy's goin' out and hav-in' fun_____ I'm
(Verse 2 see block lyrics)

just a fool for stay-in' home and hav-in' none._____ I

can't get ov-er how she set me free,_____

1.
oh,_____ lone-some me._____ 2. A

2.
me._____ I'll bet she's not like me, she's

out and fan-cy free. Flirt-ing with the boys with all her

charms._____ But I still love her so and,

bro - ther, don't you know I'd wel - come her right back here in my

arms._____ Well, there must be some way I can lose these

lone-some blues,_____ for - get a - bout the past and find some - bo - dy new.___

___ I've thought of ev - 'ry - thing from A to Z,_____

oh,_____ lone-some me.___

Verse 2:
A bad mistake I'm makin' by just hangin' 'round
I know that I should have some fun and paint the town
A lovesick fool that's blind and just can't see
Oh, lonesome me.

Rawhide

Words by Ned Washington
Music by Dimitri Tiomkin

Brightly

Roll - in' roll - in' roll - in' roll - in' roll - in' roll - in'

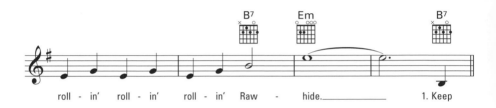

roll - in' roll - in' roll - in' Raw - hide.＿＿＿ 1. Keep

roll - in' roll - in' roll - in' though the streams are swol - len,
(Verse 2 see block lyrics)

keep them dog - gies roll - in' Raw - hide.＿＿＿ Through

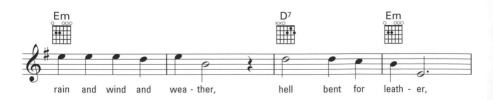

rain and wind and wea - ther, hell bent for leath - er,

wish - ing my girl is by my side,_____

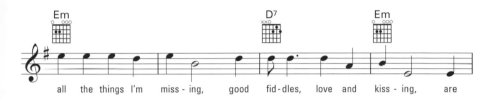

all the things I'm miss - ing, good fid - dles, love and kiss - ing, are

wait - ing at the end of my ride._____ Move 'em

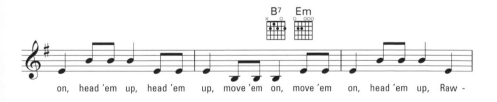

on, head 'em up, head 'em up, move 'em on, move 'em on, head 'em up, Raw -

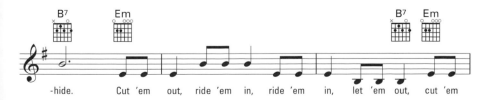

-hide. Cut 'em out, ride 'em in, ride 'em in, let 'em out, cut 'em

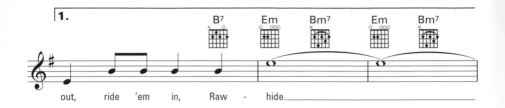

out, ride 'em in, Raw - hide.

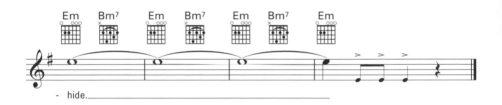

2. Keep out. Ride 'em in Raw -

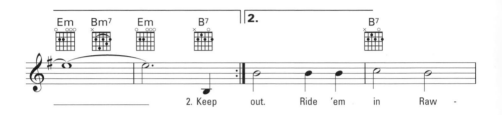

- hide.

Verse 2:
Keep movin', movin', movin'
Though they're disapprovin'
Keep them doggies moving Rawhide.
Don't try to understand 'em
Just rope 'em throw and brand 'em
Soon we'll be livin' high and wide
My heart's calculating
My true love will be waiting
Be waiting at the end of my ride.

Long Black Veil

Words & Music by Danny Dill & Marijohn Wilkin

Moderately

1. Ten years a - go,____ on a cold dark night,____ there was

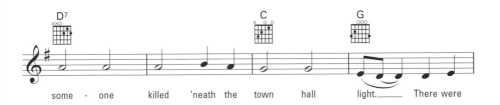

some - one killed 'neath the town hall light.____ There were

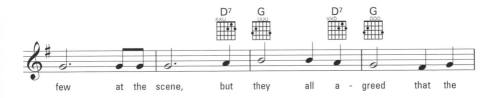

few at the scene, but they all a - greed that the

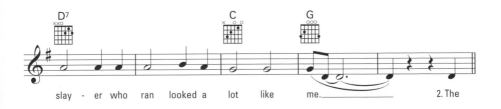

slay - er who ran looked a lot like me.____ 2. The

judge said "Son, what is your al - i - bi?____ If you were
(Verse 3 see block lyrics)

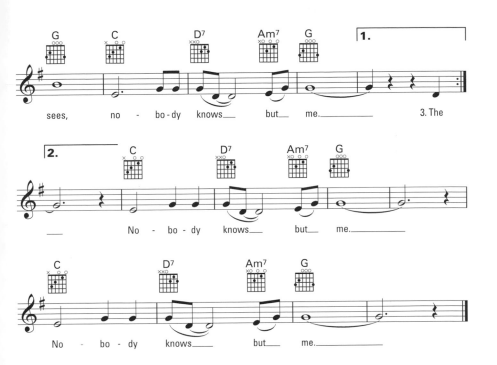

sees,   no - bo-dy   knows___   but__   me._____   3. The

No - bo - dy   knows___   but__   me._____

No - bo - dy   knows____   but__   me._____

Verse 3:
The scaffold was high and eternity near
She stood in the crowd and shed not a tear
But sometimes at night
When the cold wind moans
In a long black veil
She cries o'er my bones.

I Can't Stop Loving You

Words & Music by Don Gibson

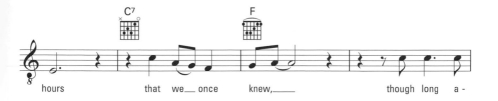

hours　　　　that we__ once　knew,____　　　　though long a -

- go,____　　　　　still make　me　blue.

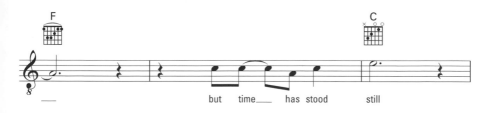

They　　say that time____　　　　heals____　a bro-ken heart__

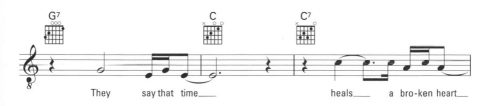

____　　　but time__ has stood　　still

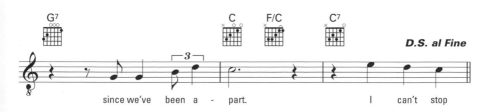

D.S. al Fine

since we've　been a - part.　　　　I　can't stop

73

He'll Have To Go

Words & Music by Joe Allison & Audrey Allison

Moderately

1. Put your sweet lips a lit-tle clo-ser to the phone, let's pre-
(Verse 2 see block lyrics)

-tend that we're to-geth-er, all a-lone. I'll tell the

man to turn the juke-box way down low, and you can

1.
tell your friend there with you, he'll have to go. 2. Whis-per

2.
hang up or will you tell him, he'll have to go. You can't

say the words I want to hear, while you're with an-oth-er man, if you

74

Verse 2:
Whisper to me tell me do you love me true
Or is he holding you the way I do?
Though love is blind, make up your mind
I've got to know, should I hang up
Or will you tell him, he'll have to go.

The 1960s was the decade when Nashville, the home of country music, often tried to smooth off even more of the rough edges that might repel radio's easy-listeners.

Marie Osmond was not really a country gal, John Denver was a hippy-dippy folk singer, Eddy Arnold was a pragmatic old-timer always ready to give the public what they wanted, and even Kenny Rogers sounded as smartly groomed as his beard looked. Yet the decade produced some undeniably interesting musical hybrids, including Marty Robbins' Pacific island-flavoured 'Devil Woman' and Sandy Posey's classic countrypolitan hit 'Single Girl'. For the purists there were still Johnny Cash, Willie Nelson, Waylon Jennings and Kris Kristofferson who could always be relied upon to provide a real country antidote to the slicker crossover hits. Some twenty years later the four of them they would form their own supergroup—The Highwaymen— to keep the country flag flying in even more parlous times. The 1960s was also the decade that gave the world Tammy Wynette's 'D-I-V-O-R-C-E' and Dolly Parton's 'Coat of Many Colors'—songs that could never belong to any genre but country.

Johnny Cash

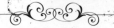

Paper Roses

Words by Janice Torre
Music by Fred Spielman

Moderately slow

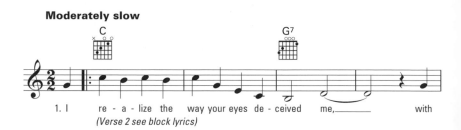

1. I re - a - lize the way your eyes de - ceived me,_____ with
(Verse 2 see block lyrics)

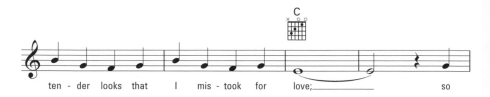

ten - der looks that I mis - took for love;_____ so

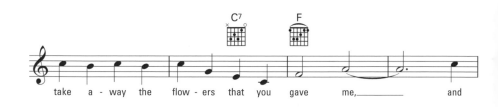

take a - way the flow - ers that you gave me,_____ and

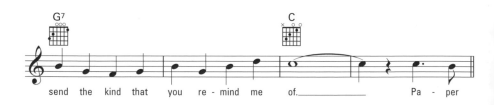

send the kind that you re - mind me of._____ Pa - per

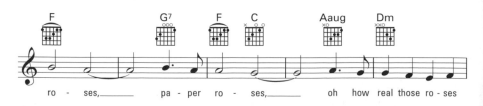

ro - ses,_____ pa - per ro - ses,_____ oh how real those ro - ses

seem to be!_____ But they're on - ly_____ im - i -

- ta - tion_____ like your im - i - ta - tion love for

1.

me._____ 2. Your

2.

me._____ Like your

im - i - ta - tion love for me._____

Verse 2:
Your pretty lips look warm and so appealing
They seem to hae the sweetness of a rose
So throw away the flowers that I gave you
I'll send the kind that you remind me of.

79

I Fall To Pieces

Words & Music by Hank Cochran & Harlan Howard

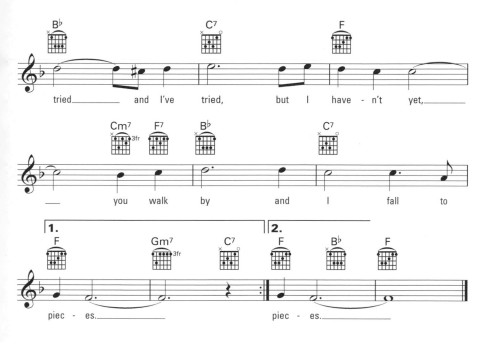

tried___ and I've tried, but I have - n't yet,___

___ you walk by and I fall to

1.
piec - es._____

2.
piec - es._____

Verse 2:
I fall to pieces, each time someone speaks your name
I fall to pieces, time only adds to the flame
You tell me to find someone else to love
Someone who'll love me too the way you used to do
But each time I go out with someone new
You walk by and I fall to pieces.

Tobacco Road

Words & Music by John D. Loudermilk

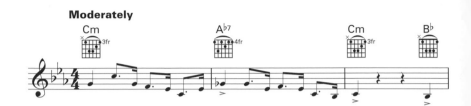

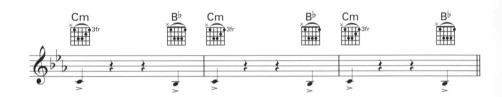

1. I was born__ in a dump, ma-ma died,__ and
(Verse 2 see block lyrics)

dad - dy got drunk. Left me here__ to die or grow,__

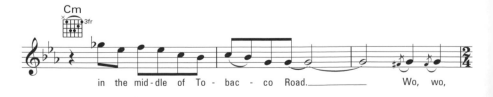

in the mid-dle of To-bac - co Road._____ Wo, wo,

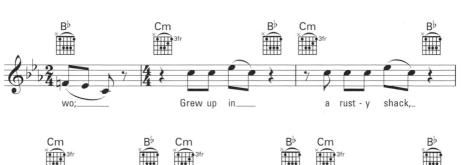

wo;_____ Grew up in____ a rust - y shack,_

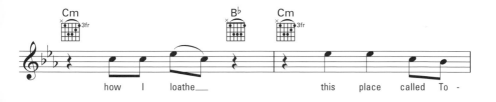

all I had was hang - in' on my back. On - ly you__ know

how I loathe____ this place called To -

-bac - co Road._____ But it's home,_____

the on - ly life I've____ ev - er known.

On - ly you_____ know how I

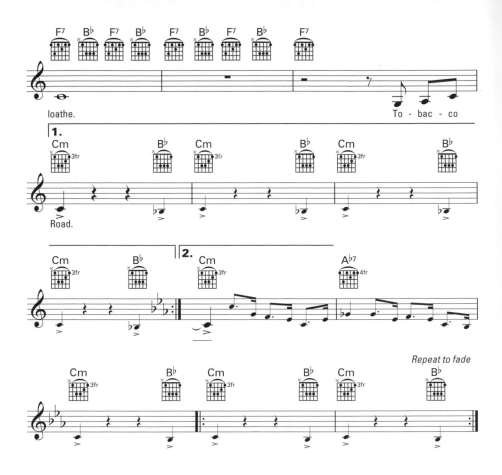

Verse 2:
Gonna leave, get a job
With the help, and the grace from above
Save some money, get rich I know
Bring it back to Tobacco Road
Wo, wo, wo
Bring dynamite, and a crane
Blow it up, start all over again
Build a town be proud to show
Give the name Tobacco Road
But it's home, the life I've ever known
I despise you 'cause you're filthy
But I love you, 'cause you're home.

Crying

Words & Music by Roy Orbison & Joe Melson

I was al - right, for a while, I could smile for a while. But I saw you last night you held my hand so tight as you stopped to say hel - lo. Oh you wished me well, you could-n't tell that I've been cry - in' ov - er you, cry - in' ov - er you. Then you said so

do_____ for you don't love me, and I'll al - ways

be, cry - in', ov- er you,__ cry - in',

ov- er you.__ Yes now you're gone and from____ this mo- ment

on, I'll be cry - in', cry - in', cry - in'

cry - in'. I'm cry - in', cry - in',

ov - - er you._____

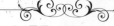

Act Naturally

Words & Music by Vonnie Morrison & Johnny Russell

Moderately

1. They're gon-na put me in the mov-ies,____
(Verses 2 & 3 see block lyrics)

they're gon-na make a big star out of me. We'll

make a scene a-bout a man that's sad and lone-ly,____ and

all I got-ta do is act nat - ural-ly. Well, I'll

bet you I'm gon - na be a big star.____ Might

win an Os-car, you can't nev-er tell; the

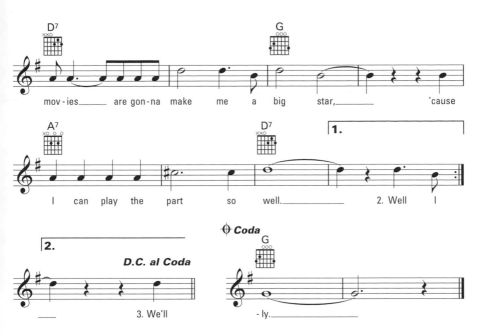

mov-ies_____ are gon-na make me a big star,_____ 'cause

I can play the part so well._____ 2. Well I

1.

2.

D.C. al Coda

_____ 3. We'll

⊕ Coda

- ly._____

Verse 2:
Well, I hope you come and see me in my movies
Then I know that you will plainly see
The biggest fool that ever hit the big time
And all I gotta do is act naturally.

Verse 3:
We'll make a scene about a man that's sad and lonely
And beggin' down upon his bended knee
I'll play the part, but I won't need rehearsin'
'Cause all I have to do is act naturally.

Big Bad John

Words & Music by Jimmy Dean

Moderately

Verse: Vamp (background for recitation)

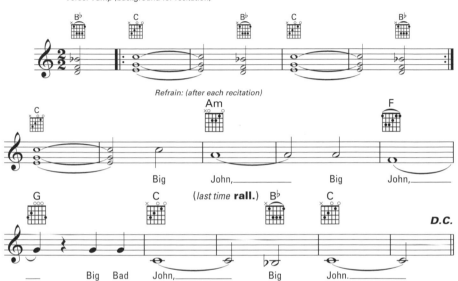

Refrain: (after each recitation)

Big   John,_____   Big   John,_____

Big   Bad   John,_____   Big   John._____

Verse 1:
Spoken:
Every morning at the mine, you could see him arrive
He stood six-foot-six, weighed two-forty-five
Kind of broad at the shoulders and narrow at the hip
And everybody knew you didn't give no lip to Big John!
(To Refrain)

Verse 2:
Nobody seemed to know where John called home
He just drifted into town and stayed all alone
He didn't say much, a-kinda quiet and shy
And if you spoke at all, you'd just said "hi" to Big John!
Somebody said he came from New Orleans
Where he got into a fight over a Cajun Queen
And a crashing a blow from a huge right hand
Sent a Lousiana fellow to the promised land. Big John!
(To Refrain)

Verse 3:
Then came the day at the bottom of the mine
When a timber cracked and men started crying
Miners were praying and hearts beat fast
And everybody thought they had breathed thier last 'cept John
Through the dust and the smoke of this man-made hell
Walked a giant of a man that the miners knew well
Grabbed a sagging timber and gave out with a groan
And like a giant oak tree, just stood there alone. Big John!
(To Refrain)

Verse 4:
And with all of his strength, he gave a mighty shove
Then a miner yelled out, "theres a light up above!"
And twenty men scrambled from a would-be grave
And now there's only one left down there to save; Big John!
With jacks and timbers, they started back down
Then came that rumble way down in the ground
And as smoke and gas belched out of that mine
Everybody knew it was the end of the line for Big John!
(To Refrain)

Verse 5:
Now they never re-opend that worthless pit
They just placed a marble stand in front of it
These few words are written on that stand:
"At the bottom of this mine, lies a big, big man; Big John!"
(To Refrain)

Crazy

Words & Music by Willie Nelson

Moderately slow

Cra - zy,_____ cra - zy for feel - in' so

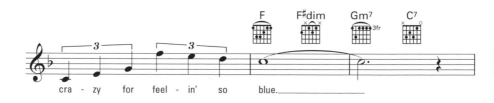

lone - ly._____ I'm cra - zy,_____

cra - zy for feel - in' so blue._____

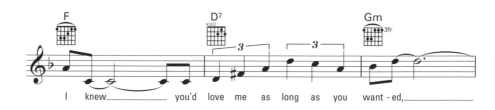

I knew_____ you'd love me as long as you want - ed,_____

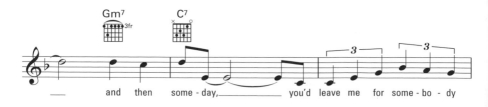

_____ and then some - day,_____ you'd leave me for some - bo - dy

I Fought The Law

Words & Music by Sonny Curtis

Moderately bright

1. A - break in' rocks in the hot sun. I fought the law and the

(Verse 2 see block lyrics)

law won. I fought the law and the law won.

I miss my ba - by and

the good fun. I fought the law and the law won.

I fought the law and the law won.

I left my ba - by and I feel so bad. I

guess my race is run. She's the best girl I've ev - er had. I fought the law and the law won. I fought the law and the law won.

2. A

Verse 2:
A-robbin' people with a zip gun
I fought the law and the law won
I fought the law and the law won
I needed money 'cause I had none
I fought the law and the law won
I fought the law and the law won.

95

Willie Nelson

Funny How Time Slips Away

Words & Music by Willie Nelson

1. Well, hel - lo there, my, it's been a long___ long time.___
(Verses 2 & 3 see block lyrics)

___ "How'm I do- in'?"___ Oh, I guess that I'm do - in' fine.___

It's been so long now___ and it seems that it was on - ly yes-ter

- day.___ Gee, ain't it fun - ny ___ how time slips a -

1, 2.
- way.___

3.
- way.___

Verse 2:
How's your new love
I hope that he's doin' fine
Heard you told him that you'd
Love him till the end of time
Now, that's the same thing that you told me
Seems like just the other day
Gee, ain't it funny how time slips away.

Verse 3:
Gotta go now
Guess I'll see you around
Don't know when though
Never know when I'll be back in town
But remember what I tell you
That in time you're gonna pay
And it's surprising how time slips away.

Hello Walls

Words & Music by Willie Nelson

Moderately

1. Hel-lo walls,_____ how'd things go for you to - day? Don't you

(Verse 2 see block lyrics)

miss her_____ since she up and walked a - way? And I'll

bet you dread to spend an - oth - er lone - ly night with me, but,

1. lone - ly walls, I'll keep you com - pa - ny._____ 2. Hel - lo,

2. rain._____ She went a - way and left us all a - lone,

the way she planned, guess we'll have to learn to get a - long with -

-out her if we can; hel-lo cei-ling,_____ I'm gon-na
stare at you a-while, you know I can't sleep,_____ so won't you
bear with me a-while? We must all pull to-geth-er, or
else I'll lose my mind, 'cause I've got a feel-in' she'll be
gone a long long time._____

Verse 2:
Hello window, well, I see that you're still here
Aren't you lonely since our darling disappeared?
Well, look here, is that a teardrop in the corner of your pane?
Now, don't you try to tell me that it's rain.

Devil Woman

Words & Music by Marty Robbins

1. I told Ma-ry a-bout_ us, I told her a-bout_ our great
(Verse 2 see block lyrics)

sin. Ma-ry cried_ and for-gave_ me and

Ma-ry took me back a - gain._ Said if I want-ed my

free-dom, I_ could be free_ ev-er more. But I don't wan-na be,

and I don't wan-na see Ma-ry cry_ a-ny more, oh._ De-vil

B   E

wo-man,__   de-vil wo-man let___ go of me.   De-vil wo-man,

B   **1-3.**   E

let   me   be,___   and   leave me   a - lone,___   I   wan-na   go   home.__

4.   E

leave me   a - lone,___   I'm   go - ing   back   home.__

Verse 2:
Mary is waiting and weeping
Down in our shack by the sea
Even after I hurt her
Mary's still in love with me
Devil woman it's over
Trapped no more by your charm
'Cause I don't want to stay
I wanna get away
Woman let go of my arm, oh.

Verse 3 :
Devil woman you're evil
Like the dark coral reef
Like the winds that bring high tides
You bring sorrow and grief
You made me ashamed to face Mary
Barely had the strength to tell
Skies are not so black
Mary took me back
Mary has broken your spell.

Verse 4:
Running along by the seashore
Running as fast as I can
Even the seagulls are happy
Glad I'm coming home again
Never again will I ever
Cause another tear to fall
Down the beach I see
What belongs to me
The one I want most of all.

She Thinks I Still Care

Words & Music by Dickey Lee

Just be-cause I ask a friend a - bout__ her,__ just be-cause I spoke her name__ some - where. Just be-

-cause I saw her then went all to piec - es, she__ thinks I still care. But,

if she's__ hap-py think-in' __ I still miss her,__ then

let that__ sil - ly no - tion__ bring her cheer.

How____ could she ev-er be____ so fool-ish,____ oh

where____ would she get such an i - de - a?

Just be-cause I haunt the same___ old pla - ces,_____ where the

mem-'ry_____ of her lin - gers____ ev-'ry - where._____ Just be -

D.S. al Coda

Coda

Just be-cause I saw her then went all to piec - es,_____

she thinks I still care._____

103

Ring Of Fire

Words & Music by Merle Kilgore & June Carter

1. Love___ is a burn - ing thing,___

(Verse 2 see block lyrics)

___ and it makes___ a fir - 'y

ring.___ Bound___

___ by wild de - sires.___

Verse 2:
The taste of love is sweet
When hearts like ours beat
I fell for you like a child
Oh, but the fire went wild.

Jackson

Words & Music by Jerry Leiber & Billy Edd Wheeler

1. We got mar - ried in a fev - er, hot-ter than a pep-per sprout.
(Verse 3 see block lyrics)

We've been talk - in' 'bout Jack - son ev - er since the fire went out.___ I'm goin' to Jack-son, I'm gon-na mess a - round,___ yeah, I'm goin' to Jack-son, look out Jack - son town.___ 2. Well go on down to
(Verse 4 see block lyrics)

Jack-son, go a-head and wreck your health. Go play your hand, ya

big talk-in' man, make a big fool of your-self,___ yeah yeah,___ go to

Jack-son, but go comb your hair.___

Go and snow-ball Jack-son, go a-head and see if I

care.___ 3. When fan.___

Verse 3:
When I breeze in to that city
People gonna stoop and bow
All them women goin' beg me
Teach 'em what they don't know how.
I'm goin' to Jackson
You turn aloose my coat
'Cause I'm goin' to Jackson
"Goodbye," that's all she wrote.

Verse 4:
They'll laugh at you in Jackson
I'll be dancin' on a pony keg
They'll lead you 'round town, a scolded hound
With your tail tucked 'tween your legs
Yeah, yeah go to Jackson
You big talkin' man
I'll be waitin' in Jackson
Behind my Japan fan.

The End Of The World

Words by Sylvia Dee
Music by Arthur Kent

Moderately

Capo fret 1

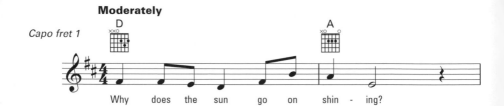

Why does the sun go on shin - ing?

Why does the sea rush to shore? Don't they know it's the

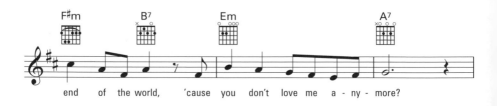

end of the world, 'cause you don't love me a - ny - more?

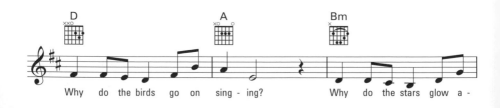

Why do the birds go on sing - ing? Why do the stars glow a -

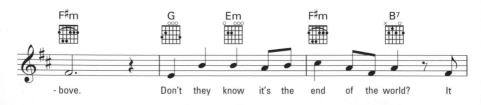

- bove. Don't they know it's the end of the world? It

end-ed when I lost your love. I wake up in the morn-ing and I

won - der why ev - 'ry-thing's the same as it was, I

can't un-der-stand, no I can't un-der-stand how life goes on the way it

does! Why does my heart go on beat - ing?

Why do these eyes of mine cry? Don't they know it's the

end of the world? It end - ed when you said good - bye.

Busted

Words & Music by Harlan Howard

In a lazy style

1. My bills are all due and the ba-by needs shoes and I'm bust-ed,____
(Verse 2 see block lyrics)

____ cot-ton is down to a quar-ter of a pound, but I'm

bust-ed.____ I've got a cow that went dry, and a

hen that won't lay. A big stack of bills that gets big-ger each day. The

1.

Coun-ty is gon-na haul my be-long-ings a-way, 'cause I'm bust-ed.____

2.

2. I bust-ed.____ Well,

I am no thief, but a man can go wrong when he's bust-ed.____

____ The food that we canned__ last sum-mer is gone, and I'm

bust-ed._____ The fields are all bare, and the cot-ton won't grow.

Me and my fam-'ly got to pack up and go, but I'll make a liv-ing, just

where I don't know, 'cause I'm bust-ed._____

Verse 2:
I went to my brother to ask for a loan, I was busted
I hate to beg like a dog without its bone, but I'm busted
My brother said there ain't a thing I can do
My wife and kids are all down with the 'flu
And I was thinking about calling on you, 'cause I'm busted.

Make The World Go Away

Words & Music by Hank Cochran

Slowly with feeling

1. Do you re - mem - ber when you loved me,
(Verse 2 see block lyrics)

be - fore the world took me a - stray.

If you do, then for - give me, and make the world go a -

- way.

Make the world go a -

- way. And get it off my

shoul - ders. Say the things you used to

say, and make the world go a - way.

1.
To Coda ⊕

2.

Make the world go a - way. 2. I'm sor - ry if I

D.S. al Coda

⊕ **Coda**

- way.

Verse 2:
I'm sorry if I hurt you
I'll make it up day by day
Just say you love me like you used to
And make the world go away.

113

Distant Drums

Words & Music by Cindy Walker

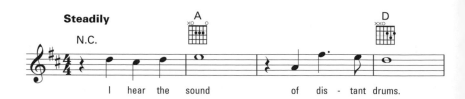

I hear the sound of dis - tant drums.

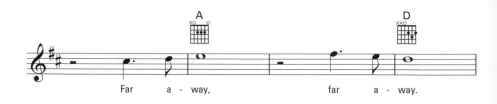

Far a - way, far a - way.

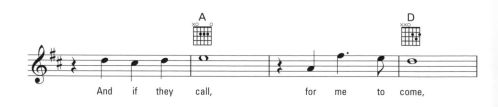

And if they call, for me to come,

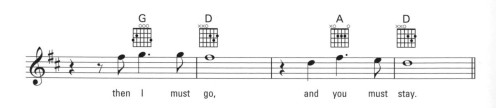

then I must go, and you must stay.

So Ma - ry mar - ry me let's not wait,

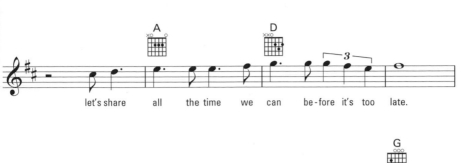

let's share all the time we can be-fore it's too late.

Love me now for now is all the time there may be.

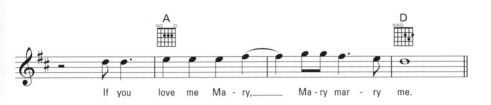

If you love me Ma - ry,_____ Ma - ry mar - ry me.

I hear the sound, of bug - les blow.

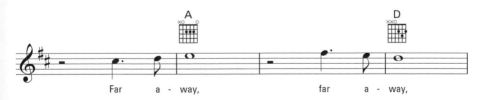

Far a - way, far a - way,

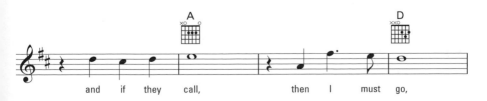

and if they call, then I must go,

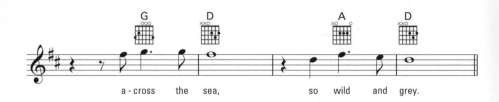

a - cross　the　sea,　　　so　wild　and　grey.

So　Ma - ry　mar - ry　me　　let's　not　wait,

for the　dis - tant drums　might change　our wed - ding　day.

Love　me　now　for　now　is　all　the time there may

be.　　If　you　love　me　Ma - ry,_____

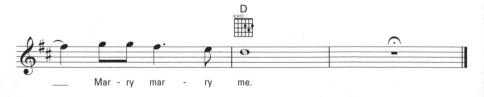

_____ Mar - ry　mar - ry　me.

Gone, Gone, Gone (Done Moved On)

Words & Music by Don Everly & Phil Everly

Fast, brightly

Capo fret 1

1. (D.C.) Some sun-ny day____ ba - by, when
(Verses 2 & 3 see block lyrics)

ev - 'ry-thing seems O. K.____ ba - by, you'll wake up and find____

____ that you're a - lone.____ 'Cause I'll be gone.____

Gone, gone, gone.____

Real - ly gone.____ Gone, gone, gone.____

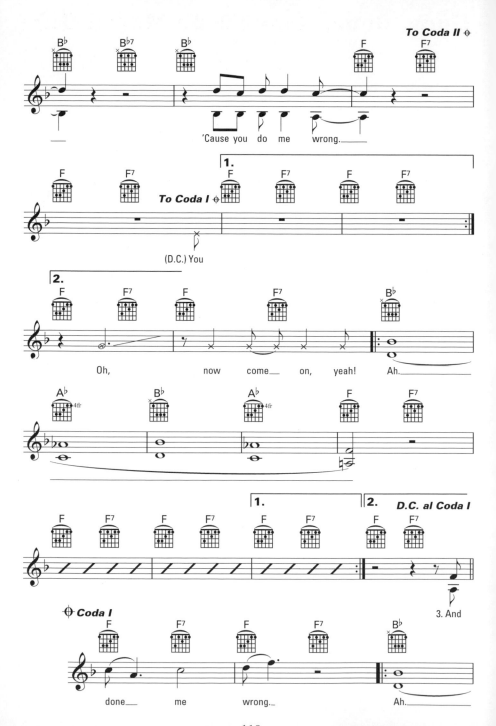

'Cause you do me wrong.

1.

To Coda I

(D.C.) You

2.

Oh, now come on, yeah! Ah.

1. **2.** D.C. al Coda I

3. And

Coda I

done me wrong. Ah.

118

D.C. al Coda II

Coda II

You done me wrong.___

Repeat with vocal ad lib.

You done me wrong.___

Verse 2:
Everyone that you meet baby
As you walk down the street baby
Will ask you why you're walking all alone
And why you're on your own
Just say I'm gone, gone, gone, gone,
Gone, gone, gone, 'cause you do me no wrong.

Verse 3:
If you change your way baby
You might get back to stay baby
You'd better hurry up, you don't want to be alone
Or I'll be gone
Just say I'm gone, gone, gone, gone,
Gone, gone, gone, 'cause you do me no wrong.

Until It's Time For You To Go

Words & Music by Buffy Sainte-Marie

Slow waltz

1. You're not a dream, you're not an an-gel, you're a
(Verses 2 & 3 see block lyrics)

man._____ I'm not a queen, I'm a

wo-man, take my hand._____ We'll make a

space in the lives that we planned,_____ and here we'll

1.
stay un-til it's time for you to go._____ 2. Yes, we're

2.
go._____

3.
go._____

Fine

120

D.S. al Fine

Don't ask why,_____

Don't ask how,_____

Don't ask for ev - er,_____

Love me now._____ 3. This love of

Verse 2:
Yes, we're diff'rent worlds apart we're not the same
We laughed and played at the start like in a game
You could have stayed outside my heart but in you came
And here you'll stay until it's time for you go.

Verse 3:
This love of mine had no beginning it has no end
I was an oak, now I'm a willow now I can bend
And though I'll never in my life see you again
Still I'll say until it's time for you to go.

Funny, Familiar, Forgotten Feelings

Words & Music by Mickey Newbury

Moderately

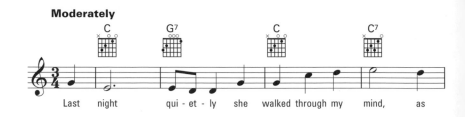

Last night qui - et - ly she walked through my mind, as

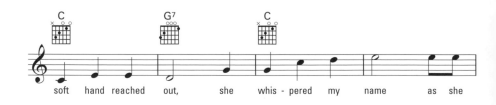

I lay search - ing for sleep,_____ her

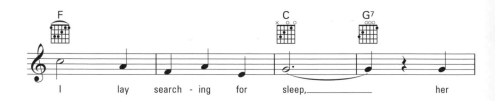

soft hand reached out, she whis - pered my name as she

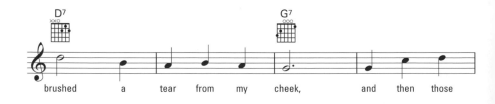

brushed a tear from my cheek, and then those

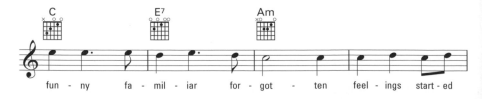

fun - ny fa - mil - iar for - got - ten feel - ings start - ed

walk - in' all ov - er my mind._____ It's

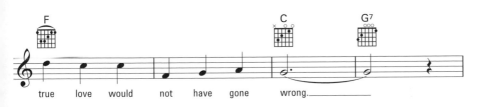

sad, so sad to watch love go bad, but a

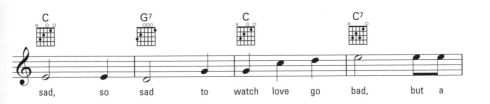

true love would not have gone wrong._____

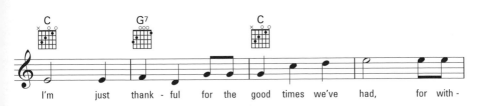

I'm just thank - ful for the good times we've had, for with -

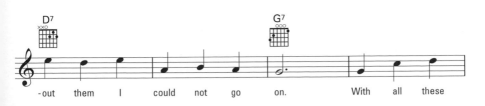

-out them I could not go on. With all these

123

funny familiar forgotten feelings walkin' all over my mind, I must go on, be strong though a million tear drops may fall, before these funny familiar forgotten feelings stop walkin' all over my mind.

Single Girl

Words & Music by Martha Sharp

Moderately

Capo fret 1

1. The sin-gle girl,___
(Verse 2 see block lyrics)

all a - lone___ in a great big town.___ The

sin-gle girl,___ gets so tired___ of love let-tin' her down.___ The

The life's un - real___ and the peo-ple are phon - y,

and then nights can get so lone - ly, the

sin-gle girl___ needs a sweet lov-in' man___ to lean on.

I've got to make my own_ way.___ There's
rent I got - ta pay,___ how I need a
night - time_ love,___ to get me through the day;_____ I'm a
sin - gle girl,___ all a - lone_ in a great big town._
I'm a sin - gle girl,___ and I get so tired_ of love
let - tin' me down;_____ but there's a man_ I've

yet to know,— wait-ing some where I've yet to go.— Some

day I'll have—— a sweet lov - in' man—— to lean
sin - gle girl—— needs a sweet lov - in' man—— to lean

1. **2.**

on.
on

The

Verse 2:
I'm a single girl,
Wondrin' if love could be passin' me by
I'm a single girl and I know all about men and their lies
Nobody loves me 'cause nobody knows me
Nobody takes the time to go slowly
The single girl needs a sweet lovin' man to lean on

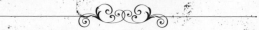

Ruby, Don't Take Your Love To Town

Words & Music by Mel Tillis

1. You have paint-ed up your lips and rolled and curled your tint-ed hair.____

(Verses 2 & 3 see block lyrics)

Ru-by, are you con-tem-plat-ing go-ing out some-where?____ The

sha-dows on the wall tell me the sun is go-ing down.____ Oh,

Ru - - - by,____ don't take your love to

town,____ for it was-n't me that start-ed that old cra-zy As-ia

war,____ but I was proud to go and do my pa-tri-ot-ic

chores._____ Oh, I know, Ru - by, that I'm not the man I used to be._____ But, Ru - - by,_____ I still need your com - pa - ny._____ 1. It's - ny_____ for
2. She's
God's sake turn a - round, don't take your love to town._____

Verse 2:
It's hard to love a man whose legs are bent and paralized
And the wants and the needs of a woman your age Ruby, I realize
But it won't be long I've heard them say until I'm not around.

Verse 3:
She's leaving now 'cause I just heard the slamming of a door
The way I know I've heard it slam one hundred times before
And if I could move I'd get my gun and put her in the ground.

I'd Rather Be Sorry

Words & Music by Kris Kristofferson

1. If you hurt me you won't be the first or the
(Verse 2 see block lyrics)

last, in a life - time of ma - ny mis -

- takes,_____ but I won't spend to -

-mor - row re - gret - ting the past, for the

chan - ces that I did - n't take._____ 'Cause

I'll nev - er know till it's ov - er,_____

Verse 2:
When you touch me it's easy to make me believe
Tomorrow won't take you away
But I'd gamble whatever tomorrow might bring
For the love that I'm living today.

Leaving On A Jet Plane

Words & Music by John Denver

1. All my bags are packed, I'm rea-dy to go, I'm stand-ing here out-

(Verses 2 & 3 see block lyrics)

-side your door, I hate to wake you up to say good -

- bye. But the dawn is break - in', it's ear - ly morn, the

tax - i's wait - in', he's blow - in' his horn, al - rea - dy I'm so

lone - some I could cry. So kiss me and

smile for me, tell me that you'll wait for me,

Verse 2:
Many times I've let you down
So many times I've played around
I tell you now they don't mean a thing
Every place I go, I'll think of you
Every song I sing, I'll sing for you
When I come back, I'll bring your wedding ring.

Verse 3:
Now the time has come to leave you
One more time let me kiss you
Then close your eyes, I'll be on my way
Dream about the days to come
When I won't have to leave alone
About the times, I won't have to say.

Ode To Billy Joe

Words & Music by Bobbie Gentry

1. It was the third of June, an-oth-er sleep-y, dust-y, del-ta day.

(Verses 2-5 see block lyrics)

I was out chop-pin' cot-ton and my bro-ther was ba-lin' hay;

and at din-ner time we stopped and walked back to the house to

eat. And Ma-ma hol-lered at the back door,"Y'all re-mem-ber to wipe your feet."

Then she said,"I got some news this morn-

-in' from Choc-taw Ridge. To-day Bil-ly Joe Mc-A-lis-ter jumped

134

off the Tal - la - hat - chee bridge."

Verse 2:
Papa said to Mama, as he passed around the black-eyed peas
"Well, Billy Joe never had a lick o' sense, pass the biscuits, please
There's five more acres in the lower forty I've got to plow"
And Mama said it was shame about Billy Joe anyhow
Seems like nothin' ever comes to no good up on Choctaw Ridge
And now Billy Joe MacAllister's jumped off the Tallahatchee Bridge.

Verse 3:
Brother said he recollected when he and Tom and Billy Joe
Put a frog down my back at the Carroll County picture show
And wasn't I talkin' to him after church last Sunday night
I'll have another piece of apple pie, you know, it don't seem right
I saw him at the sawmill yesterday on Choctaw Ridge
And now you tell me Billy Joe's jumped off the Tallahatchee Bridge.

Verse 4:
Mama said to me, "Child, what's happened to your appetite?
I been cookin' all mornin' and you haven't touched a single bite
That nice young preacher Brother Taylor dropped by today
Said he'd be pleased to have dinner on Sunday, oh, by the way
He said he saw a girl that looked a lot like you up on Choctaw Ridge
And she an' Billy Joe was throwin' somethin' off the Tallahatchee Bridge."

Verse 5:
A year has come and gone since we heard the news 'bout Billy Joe
Brother married Becky Thompson, they bought a store in Tupelo
There was a virus goin' 'round, Papa caught it and he died last Spring
And now Mama doesn't seem to wanna do much of anything
And me I spend a lot of time pickin' flowers up on Choctaw Ridge
And drop them into the muddy water off the Tallahatchee Bridge.

Gentle On My Mind

Words & Music by John Hartford

Moderately bright

1. It's know-ing that your door is al-ways op-en and your path is free to
(Verses 2 -4. see block lyrics)

walk,_____ that

makes me tend to leave my sleep-ing bag rolled up and stashed be - hind your

couch._____ And it's

know-ing I'm not shack-led by for - got-ten words and bonds,_ and the

ink stains that have dried up - on some line,_____

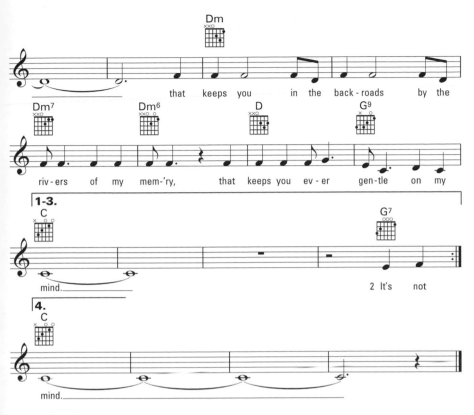

Dm

that keeps you in the back-roads by the

Dm⁷   **Dm⁶**   **D**   **G⁹**

riv-ers of my mem-'ry, that keeps you ev-er gen-tle on my

1-3.
C   **G⁷**

mind. 2 It's not

4.
C

mind.

Verse 2:
It's not clinging to the rocks and ivy planted on their columns now that binds me
Or something that somebody said because they thought we fit together walkin'
It's just knowing that the world will not be cursing or forgiving
When I walk along some railroad track and find
That you are moving on the backroads by the rivers of my mem'ry
And for hours you're just gentle on my mind.

Verse 3:
Though the wheat fields and the clothes lines and the junkyards and the highways come between us
And some other woman crying to her mother 'cause she turned and I was gone
I still might run in silence, tears of joy might stain my face
And the summer sun might burn me 'til I'm blind
But not to where I cannot see you walkin' on the backroads
By the rivers flowing gentle on my mind.

Verse 4:
I dip my cup of soup back from the gurglin' cracklin' caldron in some train yard
My beard a roughing coal pile and a dirty hat pulled low across my face
Through cupped hands 'round a tin can I pretend
I hold you to my breast and find
That you're waving from the backroads by the rivers of my mem'ry
Ever smilin', ever gentle on my mind.

Just Dropped In
(To See What Condition
My Condition Was In)

Words & Music by Mickey Newbury

Moderately

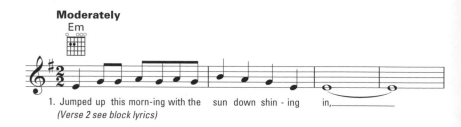

1. Jumped up this morn-ing with the sun down shin - ing in,
(Verse 2 see block lyrics)

found my bro-ken mind in a brown pa-per bag, but then,_____ I

tripped on a cloud and fell eight miles high,_ Tore my mind on the jag-ged sky._ I

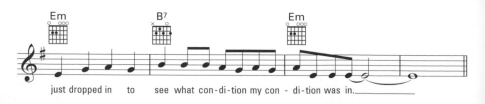

just dropped in to see what con-di-tion my con - di-tion was in._____

Verse 2:
Someone painted, "April fool" in big black letters on a dead-end sign
I had my foot on the gas as I left the road and blew out my mind
Eight miles out of Memphis and I got no spare
Eight miles straight up downtown somewhere
I just dropped in to see what condition my condition was in.

Wichita Lineman

Words & Music by Jimmy Webb

I am a line man for the coun-ty___ and I drive the main road search-in' in the sun for an-oth-er___ ov - er load. I hear you sing-in' in the wi-res___ I can hear you through the whine___ and the Wi - chi-ta line___ man___ is still on the line. ___ I know I need a small va - ca - tion,

but it don't look like rain, and if it snows, that stretch down south will

nev - er___ stand___ the strain and I need you more than

want you,___ and I want you for all time___

and the Wi - chi - ta Line - man___ is still on the

line.___

Repeat to fade

141

For The Good Times

Words & Music by Kris Kristofferson

Moderately

Capo fret 1

1. Don't look so sad_____ I know it's
(Verse 2 see block lyrics)

ov - er, _____ but life goes on_____ and this old

world_____ will keep on turn - ing._____ Let's just be

glad_____ we had some time_____ to spend to - geth - er,_____

_____ there's no need_____ to watch the brid- ges_____ that we're burn - ing._____

_____ Lay your head_____ up - on my pil - low,

142

hold your warm_____ and ten-der bo-dy_____ close to mine._____

Hear the whis-per_____ of the rain-drops_____ blow-ing soft_____ a-gainst the

win-dow_____ and make be-lieve you love me one more time._____

For the good times. 2. I'll get a- For the

good times,_____ for the good times._____

Verse 2:
I'll get along you'll find another
But I'll be here if you should find you ever need me
Don't say a word about tomorrow or forever
There'll be time enough for sadness when you leave me.

143

Kris Kristofferson

Daddy Sang Bass

Words & Music by Carl Perkins

1. I re - mem-ber when I was a lad, times were hard and things were
(Verse 2 see block lyrics)

bad, but there's a sil - ver lin - ing be - hind ev - 'ry

cloud._____ Just poor peo-ple that's all we were try'n to make a

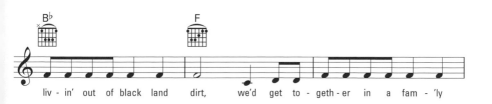

liv - in' out of black land dirt, we'd get to - geth - er in a fam - 'ly

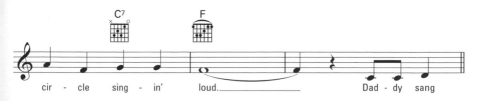

cir - cle sing - in' loud._____ Dad - dy sang

bass, ma - ma sang ten - or, me and lit - tle bro - ther would join right

in there, sing - in' seems to help a trou - bled

soul.___ One of these days, and it won't be

long, I'll re - join them in a song, I'm gon - na

join the fam - 'ly cir - cle at the throne.___ No, the

cir - cle___ won't be bro - ken,___

___ bye and bye, Lord, bye and bye.___

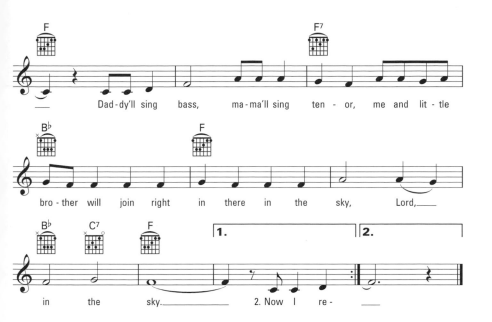

Dad-dy'll sing bass, ma-ma'll sing ten - or, me and lit - tle

bro - ther will join right in there in the sky, Lord,____

in the sky.____ 2. Now I re -

1.

2.

Verse 2:
Now I remember after work
Mama would call in all of us
You could hear us singing for a country mile
Now, little brother has done gone on
But I'll rejoin him in a song
We'll be together again
Up yonder in a little while.

Harper Valley P.T.A.

Words & Music by Tom T. Hall

1. I want to tell you all a sto - ry 'bout a
(Verse 2 see block lyrics)

Har - per Val - ley wid-owed wife,___ who had a

teen - age daugh - ter who at - ten - ded Har - per Val - ley Jun - ior

High. Well her daugh-ter came home___ one af - ter -noon___

___ and did - n't ev - en stop to play, and she said

"Ma - ma got__ a note__ here from the Har - per Val - ley P. T. A."__

1.

2. Well the ___

3. Well it hap-pened that__ the P. T. A.__ was
(Verse 4 see block lyrics)

gon-na meet__ that ve - ry af - ter - noon, and they were

sure sur - prised when Miss-es John - son wore her mi - ni skirt in - to the

room. And as she walked up to the black-board I can

still re - call__ the words she had to say, She said I'd

149

like   to   ad - dress_ this meet - ing of___ the Har - per Val - ley P. T.

1. E♭ B♭

A.___

2.

4. Well there's down.___

B

5. Well Mis - ter   Har - per could -n't be here 'cause he

stayed too long in Kel-ly's bar_ a - gain,   and if you

E

smell_ Shir - ley Thomp-son's breath you'll find she's had a lit - tle niff

B

of gin.___   And then you have the nerve_ to tell me, you

think that as___ a Moth-er I'm not fit.   Well this is

Verse 2:
Well the note say Mrs Johnson you're wearing your dresses way too high
It's reported you been drinkin' and a running round with men and going wild
And we don't believe you ought to be a-bringing up your little girl this way
And it was signed by the secretary Harper Valley P.T.A.

Verse 4:
Well there's Bobby Taylor sittin' there and seven times he's asked me for a date
And Misses Taylor sure seem to use a lotta ice whenever he's away
And Mister Baker can you tell us why your secretary had to leave this town?
And shouldn't widow Jones be told to keep her window shades all pulled completely down.

Guitar Man

Words & Music by Jerry Reed

Bright beat

Capo fret 1

1. Well I quit my job down at the car - wash, and left my
(Verse 2 see block lyrics)

ma - ma a good-bye note, By sun-down I'd left

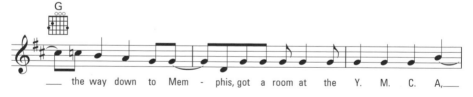

Kings - ton with my gui - tar un - der my coat. I hitch-hiked all

the way down to Mem - phis, got a room at the Y. M. C. A,

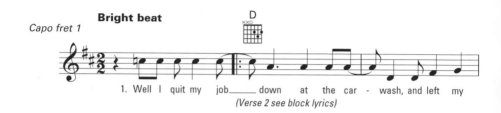

a - for the next three weeks I went a - haunt-ing them night-clubs, a -

-look-ing for a place to play. Well I thought my pick-ing would

set 'em on fire but no-bo-dy want-ed to hire a gui-tar man.

1.

Well I near-ly 'bout starved

(Spoken) We don't need a gui-tar man,

son.

So I slept in the ho-bo jun-

- gles, a-round a thou-sand miles of track,___ 'till I

found my-self in Mo - bile, Al-a-ba-ma, at at club they call "Big

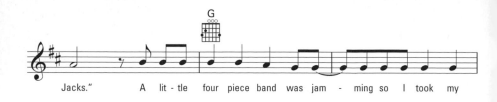

Jacks." A lit-tle four piece band was jam - ming so I took my

gui - tar and I sat in, I showed 'em what a band would

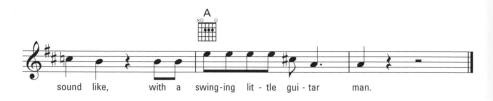

sound like, with a swing-ing lit - tle gui - tar man.

Verse 2:
Well I nearly 'bout starved to death in Memphis
I ran out of money and luck
So I bought me a ride down to Macon Georgia
On an overloaded poultry truck
I thumbed on down to Panama City
Started picking out some of them all night bars
I'm hoping I can make myself a dollar
Making music on my guitar
I got the same old story at them all night piers
That there ain't no room around here for a guitar man.

Tammy Wynette

D-I-V-O-R-C-E

Words & Music by Bobby Braddock & Curly Putman

Moderately

1. Our lit - tle boy is four years old,___ and quite a lit - tle

(Verse 2 see block lyrics)

man, so we spell___ out the___ words we___ don't want

him to un - der - stand. Like t - o - y or may - be

s - u - r - p - r - i - s - e.___ But the

words we're hid - ing from him___ now tear the heart right out___ of

me, our D - I - V - O - R - C - E

Verse 2:
Watch him smile, he thinks
It's Christmas or his fifth birthday
And he thinks c-u-s-t-o-d-y spells fun or play
I spell out all the hurtin' words
And turn my head when I speak
Because I can't spell away this hurt
That's drippin' down my cheeks.

I've Always Been Crazy

Words & Music by Waylon Jennings

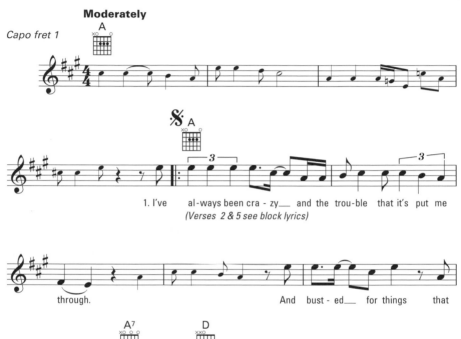

1. I've al-ways been cra - zy___ and the trou-ble that it's put me
(Verses 2 & 5 see block lyrics)

through. And bust-ed___ for things that

I did and I did-n't do. I

can't say I'm proud of all of the things that I've done.

But I can say I nev-er in-ten-tion-'ly hurt a-ny-

Verse 2:
I've always been diff'rent with one foot over the line
Windin' up somewhere one step ahead or behind
It ain't been so easy, I guess I shouldn't complain
I've always been crazy, it's kept me from goin' insane.

Verse 4:
Are you really sure, you really want what you see?
Be careful of something that's just what you want it to be.

Verse 5:
I've always been crazy, but it's kept me from goin' insane
Nobody knows if it's somethink to bless or to blame
So far I ain't found a rhyme or a reason to change
I've always been crazy, but it's kept me from goin' insane.

I'm Gonna Be A Country Girl Again

Words & Music by Buffy Sainte-Marie

Moderato

1. The rain is fall - in' light - ly on the build - ings and the

(Verses 2 & 3 see block lyrics)

cars, I've said good - bye to ci - ty friends, de -

-part - ment stores and bars. The lights of town are at my back, my

heart is full of stars, and I'm gon - na be a

coun - try girl a - gain. Oh, yes, I'm gon - na be a

coun - try girl a - gain, with an old brown dog and a

big front porch, and rab - bits in the pen. I tell you

all the lights on Broad - way don't a - mount to an a - cre of

To Coda ⊕

green, and I'm gon - na be a coun - try girl a -

1, 2.

- gain. 2. I've

3. **D.S. al Coda** ⊕ **Coda**

—— Oh, yes I'm - gain.

Verse 2:
I've spent some time in study, oh, I've taken my degrees
And memorized my formuli, my A's 'n' B's 'n' C's
But what I know came long ago and not from such as these
And I'm gonna be a country girl again.

Verse 3:
I've wandered in the hearts of men, looking for the sign
That here I might learn happiness, I might learn peace of mind
The one who taught my lesson was the south wind through the pines
And I'm gonna be a country girl again.

161

Help Me Make It Through The Night

Words & Music by Kris Kristofferson

Capo fret 1

Moderately

1. Take the rib - bon from your hair,
(Verse 2 see block lyrics)

shake it loose and let it fall,____

lay - in' soft up - on my skin,____

1.
like the sha - dows on the wall.

2, 3.
To Coda
Help me make it through the night,

D

I don't care who's right or wrong,————

G

D

I don't try to un - der - stand,————

E7

let the de - vil take to - mor - row,————

A7

D.C. al Coda

Lord, to - night I need a friend.————

𝄌 *Coda* **D** **G** **D**

night.————

Verse 2:
Come and lay down by my side
Till the early mornin' light
All I'm takin' is your time
Help me make it through the night.

163

Me And Bobby McGee

Words & Music by Kris Kristofferson & Fred Foster

Moderately

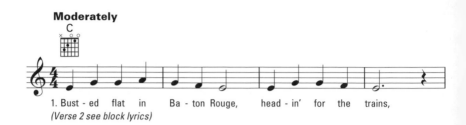

1. Bust - ed flat in Ba - ton Rouge, head - in' for the trains,
(Verse 2 see block lyrics)

feel - in' near - ly fad - ed as my jeans.

Bob - by thumbed a die - sel down just be - fore it rained,

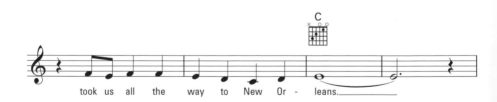

took us all the way to New Or - leans.

I took my har - poon out of my dir - ty, red bad - dan - na and was

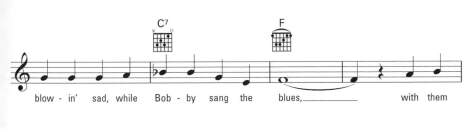
blow - in' sad, while Bob - by sang the blues,_____ with them

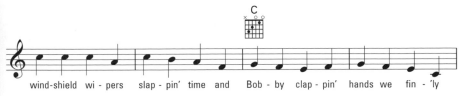
wind-shield wi - pers slap - pin' time and Bob - by clap - pin' hands we fin - 'ly

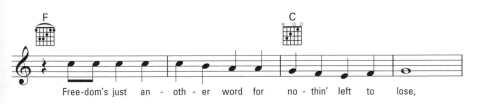
sang up ev - 'ry song that driv - er knew.

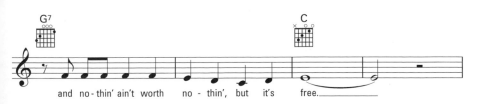
Free-dom's just an - oth - er word for no - thin' left to lose,

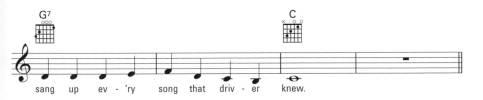
and no - thin' ain't worth no - thin', but it's free._____

Feel - ing good was ea - sy, Lord, when Bob - by sang the

blues; and, bud - dy, that was good e - nough for me,_____

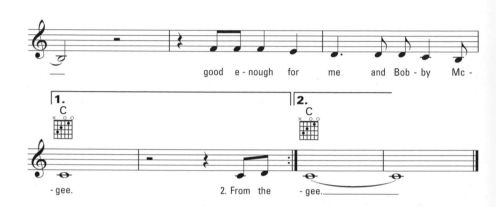

_____ good e - nough for me and Bob - by Mc -

1.
2.

- gee. 2. From the - gee._____

Verse 2:
From the coal mines of Kentucky
To the California sun
Bobby shared the secrets of my soul
Standin' right beside me Lord
Through everything I done
And every night she kept me from the cold
Then somewhere near Salinas Lord
I let her slip away
Lookin' for the home I hope she'll find
And I'd trade all my tomorrows
For a single yesterday
Holdin' Bobby's body next to mine.

Freedom's just another word
For nothin' left to lose
And nothin' left is all she left for me
Feeling good was easy Lord
When Bobby sang the blues
And, buddy, that was good enough for me
Good enough for me and Bobby McGee.

Sunday Morning Coming Down

Words & Music by Kris Kristofferson

Capo fret 1

1. Well, I woke up Sun-day morn-in' with no way to hold my head that did-n't
(Verse 2 see block lyrics)

hurt, and the beer I had for break-fast was-n't

bad, so I had one more for des - sert.____ Then I

fum-bled through my clos-et for my clothes and found my clean-est dir-ty shirt,

1.

and I shaved my face, and combed my hair, and

stum-bled down the stair to meet the day. 2. Well, I'd

2.

took me back to some-thin' that I'd lost some-how some-where a-long the way.

On the Sun-day morn-in' side-walk, wish-in', Lord, that I was

stoned, 'cause there's some-thing in a Sun - day

makes a bo - dy feel a - lone. And there's no - thin' short of

dy - in' half as lone-some as a sound,

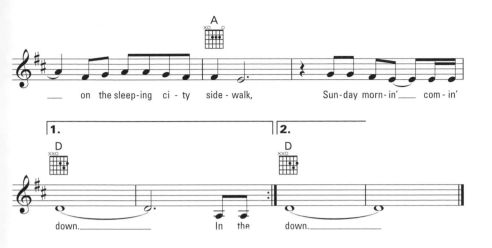

on the sleep-ing ci - ty side - walk, Sun-day morn- in'___ com - in'

down.___ In the down.___

Verse 2:
I'd smoked my brain the night before
With cigarette and songs that I'd been a-pickin'
But I lit my first and watched a small kid
Cussin' at a can that he was kickin'
Then I crossed the empty street
And caught the Sunday smell of someone fryin' chicken
And it took me back to somethin'
I'd lost somehow, somewhere along the way.

Verse 3:
In the park I saw a daddy
With a laughing little girl who he was swingin'
And I stopped beside a Sunday school
And listened to the song they were singin'
Then I headed back for home
And somewhere far away a lonely bell was ringin'
And it echoed through the canyon
Like the disappearing dreams of yesterday.

Raindrops Keep Falling On My Head

Words by Hal David
Music by Burt Bacharach

Rhythmically

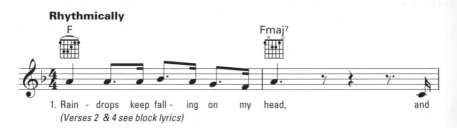

1. Rain - drops keep fall - ing on my head, and
(Verses 2 & 4 see block lyrics)

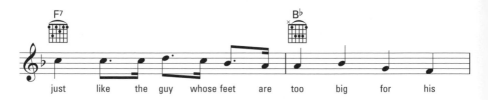

just like the guy whose feet are too big for his

bed, no - thin' seems to fit. Those rain - drops are fall - ing on my

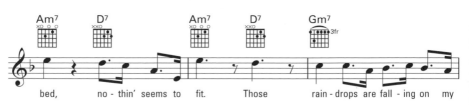

3° To Coda

head, they keep fall - ing.
2. So I just
3. But there's one thing I know,
4. Be - cause I'm

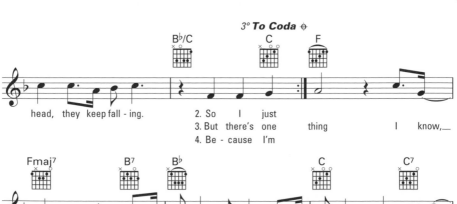

the blues__ they send__ to meet__ me won't de - feat

me. It won't be long— till hap-pi - ness— steps up—

D.C. al Coda

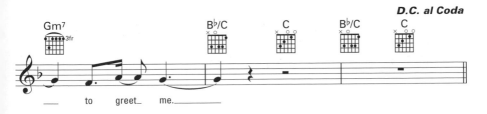

— to greet— me.—

✠ Coda

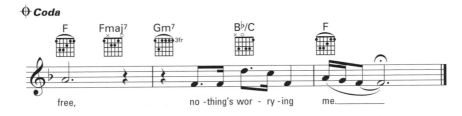

free, no -thing's wor - ry -ing me.—

Verse 2:
So I just did me some talking to the sun
And I said I didn't like the way he got things done
Sleeping on the job
Those raindrops are falling on my head
They keep falling!

Verse 4:
Raindrops keep falling on my head
But that doesn't mean my eyes will soon be turning red
Crying not for me
'Cause I'm never gonna stop the rain by complaining
Because I'm free, nothing's worrying me.

San Quentin

Words & Music by John R. Cash

Sung freely

Capo fret 1

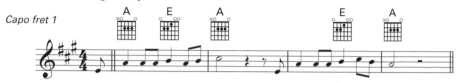

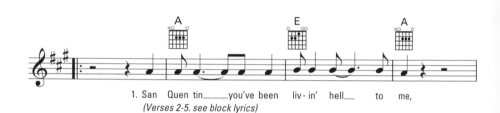

1. San Quen tin____you've been liv-in' hell__ to me,
(Verses 2-5. see block lyrics)

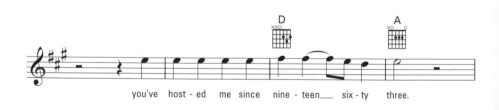

you've host - ed me since nine - teen___ six - ty three.

I've seen 'em come and go and I've seen 'em die,___

and long a-go__ I've stopped ask-ing why. San

Quen tin_____ you've been liv-ing hell to me.

Verse 2:
San Quentin I hate every inch of you
You've cut me and you've scarred me through and through
And I'll walk out a wiser weaker man
Mister congressman why can't you understand.

Verse 3:
Instrumental

Verse 4:
San Quintin what good do you think you do?
Do you think that I'll be different when you're through?
You bend my heart and mind and you warp my soul
You stone walls turn my blood a little cold.

Verse 5:
San Quintin may you rot and burn in hell
May your walls fall and may I live to tell
May all the world forget you ever stood
And the whole world will regret you did no good.

A Boy Named Sue

Words & Music by Shel Silverstein

Moderately

Capo fret 1

1. Well, my dad - dy left home when I was three,__ and he

(Verses 3, 5, 7, 9 see block lyrics)

did - n't leave much to ma and me,__ just this old gui - tar and an

emp - ty bot - tle of booze. Now I

don't blame him__ be - cause he run and hid, but the mean-est thing__ that he

ev - er did__ was be - fore he left, he went and named me Sue.

2. Well, he must have thought it was quite a joke,__ and it

(Verses 4, 6, 8, 10 see block lyrics)

got lots of laughs from a lot of folks, it seem I had to fight my whole life through. Some gal would gig-gle and I'd get red, and some guy would laugh and I'd bust his head, I tell you, life ain't ea-sy for a boy named Sue.

for repeats — *(to additional verses)* — *(last time)*

3. Well

Verse 3:
Well, I grew up quick and I grew up mean
My fist got hard and my wits got keen
Roamed from town to town to hide my shame
But I made me a vow to the moon and stars
That I'd search the honky tonks and bars
And kill that man who gave me that awful name.

Verse 4:
But it was Gatlinburg in mid July
And I just hit town and my throat was dry
I thought I'd stop and have myself a brew
At an old saloon on a street of mud
And at a table, dealing stud
Sat the dirty, mangy dog that named me Sue.

Verse 5:
Well, I knew that snake was my own sweet dad
From a worn-out picture that my mother had
And I knew that scar on his cheek and his evil eye
He was big and bent and gray and old
And I looked at him and my blood ran cold
And I said: "My name is Sue. How do you do!
Now you're gonna die"
Yeah, that's what I told him.

Verse 6:
Well, I hit him right between the eyes
And he went down, but to my surprise
He come up with a knife and cut off a piece of my ear
But I busted a chair right across his teeth
And we crashed through the wall and into the street
Kicking and a-gouging in the mud and the blood and the beer.

Verse 7:
I tell you I've fought tougher men
But I really can't remember when
He kicked like a mule and he bit like a crocodile
I heard him laughin' and then I heard him cussin'
He went for his gun and I pulled mine first
He stood there lookin' at me and I saw him smile

Verse 8:
And he said: "Son, this world is rough
And if a man's gonna make it, he's gotta be tough
And I know I wouldn't be there to help you along.
So I give you that name and I said "Goodbye,"
I knew you'd have to get tough or die
And it's the name that helped to make you strong."

Verse 9:
Yeah, he said now you have just fought one hell of a fight
And I know you hate me, and you've got the right
To kill me now, and I wouldn't blame you if you do
But you ought to thank me, before I die
For the gravel in your guts and the spit in your eye
Cause I'm the son-of-a-bitch that named you Sue.

What could I do? What could I do?

Verse 10:
I got all choked up and I threw down my gun
And I called him my pa, and he called me a son
And I came away with a different point of view
And I think about him, now and then
Every time I tried, everytime I win
And if I ever have a son, I think I'm gonna name him
Bill or George! Anything but Sue!

Coat Of Many Colors

Words & Music by Dolly Parton

Moderately

Capo fret 1

1. Back through the years I go wan-d'ring once a-gain,___

back to the sea-sons of my youth.___ I re-

-call a box of rags that some-one gave us, and

how my ma-ma put the rags___ to use.___ There were

2. rags of___ ma-ny col-ors, but___ ev-'ry piece was small, and I

(Verses 3, 5, 6. see block lyrics)

did-n't have a coat,___ and it was way down in the fall.___

177

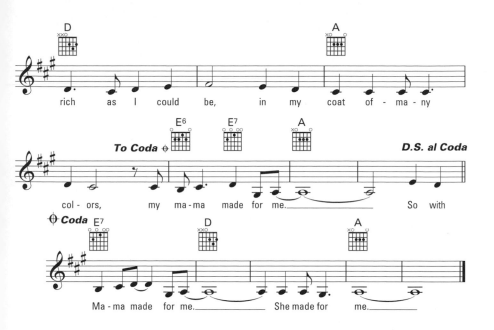

rich   as   I   could   be,   in   my   coat   of - ma - ny

To Coda col - ors,   my   ma - ma   made   for   me.＿＿＿＿   So   with   **D.S. al Coda**

Coda Ma - ma made   for   me.＿＿＿＿   She made for   me.＿＿＿＿

Verse 3:
As she sewed she told a story
From the bible she had read
'Bout a coat of many colors
Joseph wore and then she said
Perhaps this coat will bring you
Good luck and happiness
And I just couldn't wait to wear it
Mama blessed it with a kiss.

Verse 5:
So with patches on my britches
And holes in both my shoes
In my coat of many colors
I hurried off to school
Just to find the others laughing
And making fun of me
In my coat of many colors
My mama made for me.

Verse 6:
And oh I couldn't understand it
For I felt I was rich
And I told 'em of the love
My mama sewed in every stitch
And I told them all the story
Mama told me while she sewed
And how my coat of many colors
Was worth more than all their clothes.

Verse 7:
But they didn't understand it
And I tried to make them see
That one is only poor
Only if they choose to be
Now I know we had no money
But I was rich as I could be
In my coat of many colors
My mama made for me
She made just for me.

The Gig Book
70s Country Hits

The polished and the raw continued to co-exist in 1970s country

The decade started with English-born Olivia Newton-John's sudden and unexpected transformation into a country singer ('Take Me Home Country Roads') and Tony Orlando & Dawn's 'Tie A Yellow Ribbon Round The Old Oak Tree'.

Purists were getting worried, but then along came George Jones with 'Good Year for the Roses' and 'He Stopped Loving Her Today' as well as Dolly Parton with 'Jolene' and 'I Will Always Love You' (the latter to be memorably covered by Whitney Houston). Parton would later have a crossover hit with 'Islands In The Stream', a duet with Kenny Rogers (above), who had a hit in this decade with 'She Believes In Me'. Genuine country was clearly still alive and well. To reinforce the point, Charlie Daniels' barnstorming 'Devil Went Down To Georgia' was a raucous hit dominated by sawing fiddles, not swooping violins.

George Jones

A Good Year For The Roses

Words & Music by Jerry Chesnut

Moderately

1. I can hard - ly bear___ the sight of lip - stick

(Verse 2 see block lyrics)

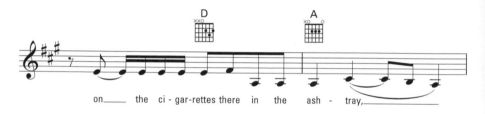

on___ the ci - gar-rettes there in the ash - tray,___

ly - ing cold the way___ you left 'em,___ but at

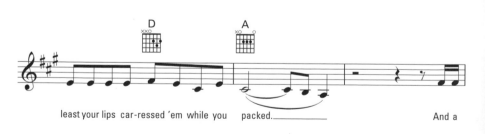

least your lips car-ressed 'em while you packed._____ And a

lip - print on a half - filled cup of cof - fee___ that you poured and did - n't

drink.___ But at least you thought you want-ed it,___ that's

so much more than I can say for me. What a good year___ for the

ro - ses,___ ma-ny blooms_ still ling-er there.

The lawn could stand an-oth-er mow-ing,

fun-ny, I___ don't ev-en care.___ As you turn to walk a-

-way,___ as the door_ be-hind you clos -

- es,   the on - ly things I have to   say,_____

it's   been a good year__ for the ros - es._____

2. Af-ter

ro - o - ses._____

Verse 2:
After three full years of marriage
It's the first time that you haven't made the bed
I guess the reason we're not talking
There's so little left to say we haven't said
While a million thoughts go racing through my mind
I find I haven't said a word
From the bedroom the familiar sound of
Our one baby's crying goes unheard.

I Recall A Gypsy Woman

Words & Music by Bob McDill & Allen Reynolds

Moderately slow

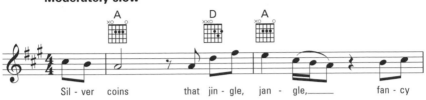

Sil - ver coins that jin - gle, jan - gle,___ fan - cy

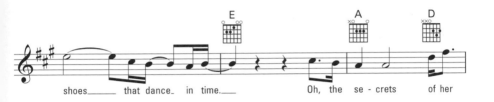

shoes___ that dance_ in time.___ Oh, the se - crets of her

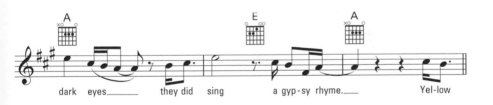

dark eyes___ they did sing a gyp-sy rhyme.___ Yel-low

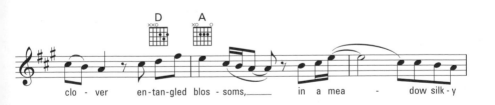

clo - ver en - tan-gled blos - soms,___ in a mea - dow silk-y

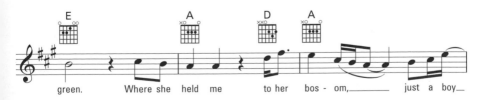

green. Where she held me to her bos - om, just a boy___

185

laugh - ter_____ and it danc - es___ in my head. While my

ten - der wife and ba - bies_____ slum-ber soft - ly in their

beds. I re- call_____ a gyp - sy wo - man, sil - ver

span - gles in her eyes. Iv - or - y skin, a-gainst the

moon - light_____ and the taste_____ of life's_ sweet wine.

(Instrumental)

Repeat to fade

187

Always On My Mind

Words & Music by Mark James, Wayne Thompson & Johnny Christopher

1. May-be I did-n't love_ you, quite as of-ten as I
3. -fied.
(Verses 2 & 3 see block lyrics)

could have._ And may-be I did-n't treat_ you,

quite as good_ as I should have. *If I made_ you feel_

_ se-cond best,_ girl I'm sor-ry I have tried._

You were al-ways on my mind, you were al-ways on my mind.

Tell me, tell me_ that your sweet love_ has-n't

Verse 2:
Maybe I didn't hold you, all those lonely, lonely times
I guess I never told you, I'm so happy that you're mine
Little things I should have said and done
I just never took the time
You were always on my mind
You were always on my mind.

Verse 3:
Instrumental till *
Little things I should have said and done
I just never took the time
You were always on my mind
You were always on my mind.

Take Me Home, Country Roads

Words & Music by John Denver, Bill Danoff & Taffy Nivert

Bright country beat

1. Al-most hea - ven,_ West Vir - gin - ia,____ Blue Ridge

(Verse 2 see block lyrics)

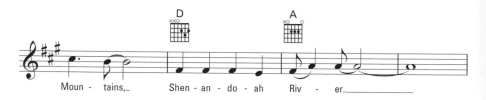

Moun - tains,_ Shen - an - do - ah Riv - er._____

Life is old there,_ old - er than the trees,

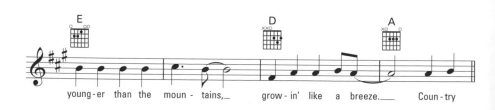

young - er than the moun - tains,_ grow - in' like a breeze.___ Coun - try

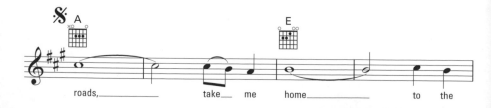

roads,_____ take__ me home_____ to the

place_____ I be - long,_____ West Vir -

-gin - ia,_____ moun - tain mom - ma,_____ take__ me

To Coda ⊕

home,_____ coun - try roads._____

1. **2.**

2. All my I hear her voice, in the

morn - in' hours she calls__ me, the ra - di - o re -

-minds me of my home far a - way, and driv - in' down the

road I get a feel - in' that I should have been home

Verse 2:
All my mem'ries gather 'round her
Miner's lady, stranger to blue water
Dark and dusty, painted on the sky
Misty taste of moonshine, teardrop in my eye.

Tie A Yellow Ribbon
'Round The Old Oak Tree

Words & Music by Irwin Levine & L. Russell Brown

Moderately bright

1. I'm com-in' home,___ I've done my time,___ now I've
(Verse 2 see block lyrics)

got to know what is___ and is-n't mine.___ If

you re-ceived my let-ter tell-in' you___ I'd soon be free,___

then you'll know just what to do___ if you still want me,

if   you   still   want   me.

Tie   a yel-low   rib-bon   round the   ole   oak   tree,___   it's   been

three   long   years,   do   ya   still   want   me?___   If

I   don't   see   a   rib-bon   round   the   ole   oak   tree___   I'll

stay on   the   bus,   for-get a-bout   us,   put   the blame on   me,   if

I   don't   see   a   yel-low   rib-bon   round   the   ole___   oak

1.

tree.___

2.

tree.＿ Now the whole damn bus is cheer-ing and I can't be-lieve I see a hun-dred yel-low rib-bons round the ole＿ oak＿ tree.＿

Verse 2:
Bus driver please look for me
'Cause I couldn't bear to see what I might see
I'm really still in prison and my love she holds the key
A simple yellow ribbon's what I need to set me free
I wrote and told her please.

Behind Closed Doors

Words & Music by Kenny O'Dell

Moderately

My ba - by makes me proud, Lord, don't she make___ me

proud, she nev - er makes a scene by hang - in'

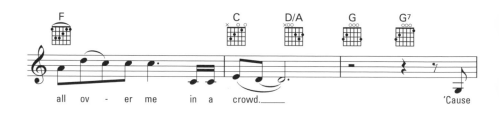

all ov - er me in a crowd.___ 'Cause

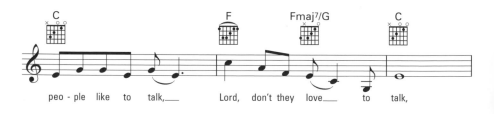

peo - ple like to talk,___ Lord, don't they love___ to talk,

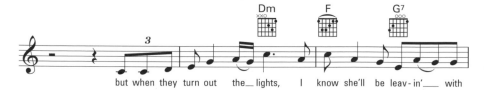

but when they turn out the___ lights, I know she'll be leav - in'___ with

196

me. And when we get be - hind closed___

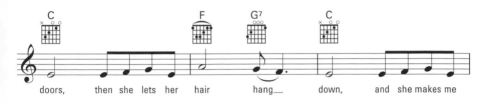

doors, then she lets her hair hang___ down, and she makes me

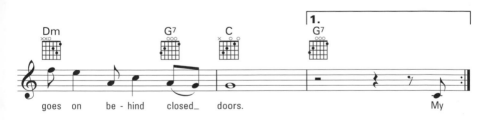

glad I'm____ a man,___ oh, no one knows what

goes on be - hind closed_ doors. My

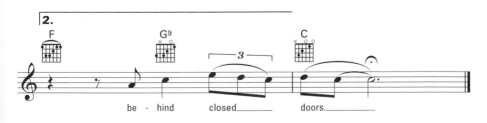

be - hind closed_____ doors._____

talks a-bout_ you in his sleep_ and there's no-thing I__ can do to keep_ from

(Verses 4-6 see block lyrics)

cry-ing when he calls your name Jo - lene._____ And

- lene, Jo - lene, Jo - lene, Jo - lene,_____

To Coda

I'm ⎧ beg - ging of you please don't take my man._____
⎩ please don't take him just be-cause you can._____

D.S. al Coda   Coda
(with repeats)

Jo -
1. Your

can._____

Jo - lene._____   Jo - lene._____

Verse 2:
Your smile is like a breath of spring
Your voice is soft like summer rain
And I cannot compete with you
Jolene.

Verse 5:
You could have your choice of men
But I could never love again
He's the only one for me
Jolene.

Verse 4:
And I can eas'ly understand
How you could eas'ly take my man
But you don't know what he means to me
Jolene.

Verse 6:
I had to have this talk with you
My happiness depends on you
And whatever you decide to do
Jolene.

199

Annie's Song

Words & Music by John Denver

Moderately

1. You fill up my sen - ses____ like a
(Verse 2 see block lyrics)

night in the for - est,____ like the

moun - tains in spring - time,____ like a walk in the

rain.____ 2. Like a storm in the

fill me a - gain.____ 3. Come let me

200

love   you,_____   let   me   give   my   life
(Verse 4 see block lyrics)

to   you,_____   let   me   drown   in   your

laugh - ter,_____   let   me   die   in   your

arms._____   Let   me   lay   down   be -

- side   you,_____   let   me   al - ways   be

with   you,_____   come   let   me

201

Verse 2:
Like a storm in the desert
Like a sleepy blue ocean
You fill up my senses
Come fill me again.

Verse 4:
You fill up my senses
Like a night in a forest
Like the mountains in springtime
Like a walk in the rain.

Like a storm in the desert
Like a sleepy blue ocean
You fill up my senses
Come fill them again.

Blanket On The Ground

Words & Music by Roger Bowling

Moderately

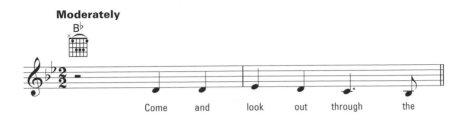

Come and look out through the

win- dow,_____ that big old moon is shin- ing

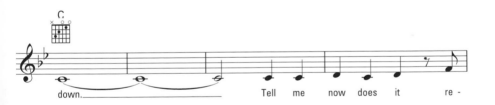

down._____ Tell me now does it re-

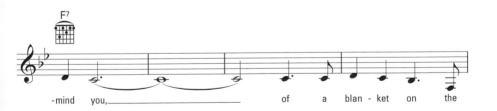

-mind you,_____ of a blan- ket on the

ground?_____ Re-mem- ber back____ when love first

found us,_____ we'd go slip - pin' out of

town,_____ and we loved__ be - neath the

moon - light,_____ on a blan - ket on the

ground._____ I'll get the blan - ket from the

bed - room,_____ and we'll go walk - in' once a -

- gain,_____ to that spot down by the

riv - er,_____ where our sweet__ love first__ be -

- gan._____ Just be - cause we are

mar - ried,_____ don't mean we can't sleep a -

- round.__ So let's walk__ out through the

moon - light,_____ and lay the blan - ket on the

1.   **2.**

ground._____

205

Dolly Parton

I Will Always Love You

Words & Music by Dolly Parton

Slow Ballad

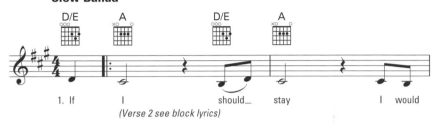

1. If   I   should__ stay   I   would

(Verse 2 see block lyrics)

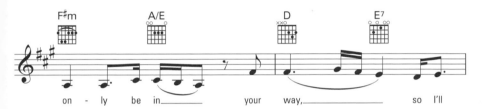

on - ly   be in_____ your   way,_____ so I'll

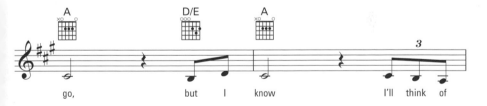

go,   but   I   know   I'll think of

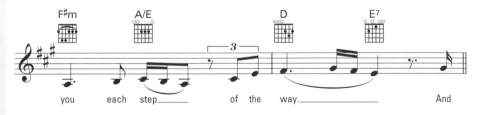

you   each   step_____ of   the way._____ And

I_____ will   al - ways__ love

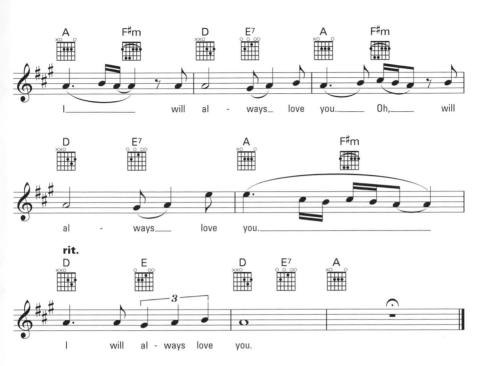

I _____ will al - ways_ love you._____ Oh,_____ will

al - ways_____ love you._____

rit.

I will al - ways love you.

Verse 2:
Bittersweet memories
That's all I am taking with me
Goodbye, please don't cry
We both know that I'm not what you need.

Let Your Love Flow

Words & Music by Larry E. Williams

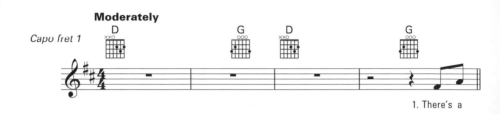

1. There's a

rea - son   for the sun - shined sky,_____ and there's a   rea -
(Verses 2 & 3 see block lyrics)

- son,_____   why I'm   feel - in' so high___ must be the sea -

- son   when that   love light shines_____ all a - round

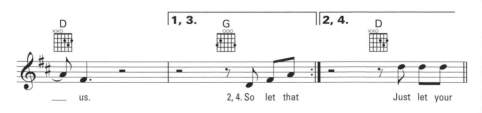

___ us.   2, 4. So   let that   Just let your

210

love flow_____ like a moun-tain stream__ and let your love

_____ grow__ with the small - est of dreams and let your love__

_____ show__ and you'll know what I mean,__ it's the sea -

- son. Let your love fly_____ like a

bird on a wing_____ and let your love__ bind you__ to

all liv-ing things__ and let your love_____ shine__ and you'll

D.S. al Coda
(with repeat)

To Coda ⊕

know what I___ mean, that's the rea - son. 3. There's a

⊕ **Coda**

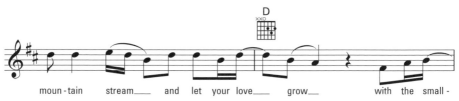

Just let your love flow_____ like a

moun - tain stream___ and let your love___ grow___ with the small -

- est of dreams_ and let your love___ show___ and you'll

know what I mean,___ it's the sea - son.

Let your love fly_____ like a

212

bird on a wing____ and let your love____ bind you____ to

all liv - ing things____ and let your love____ shine____ and you'll

Repeat to fade

know what I____ mean, that's the rea - son.   Just let your

Verse 2:
So let that feelin' grab you deep inside
And send you reelin' where your love can't hide
And then those feelings through the moonlit nights
With your lover.

Verse 3:
There's a reason for the warm sweet nights
And there's a reason for the candle lights
Must be the season when those love rites shine
All around us.

Verse 4:
So let that wonder take you into space
And lay you under its loving embrace
Just feel the thunder as it warms your face
You can't hold back.

Talking In Your Sleep

Words & Music by Roger Cook & Bobby Wood

Moderately slow

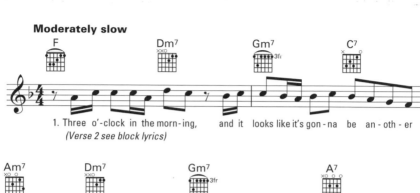

1. Three o'-clock in the morn-ing, and it looks like it's gon-na be an-oth-er
(Verse 2 see block lyrics)

sleep-less night.   I've been list-'nin' to your dreams and get-tin' ve-ry

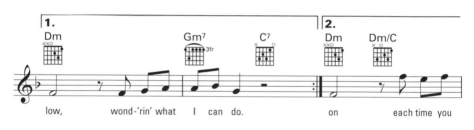

1. low,   wond-'rin' what I can do.   **2.** on   each time you

close your eyes.   I've heard it said that dream-ers nev-er lie.

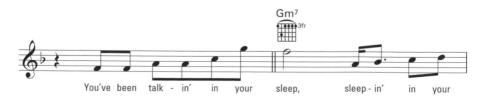

You've been talk-in' in your sleep,   sleep-in' in your

dreams, with some— sweet lov - er. Hold - in' on so tight, lov - in' him the way you used to love me.

Talk - in' in your sleep with lov - in' on your mind.___

___ You've been talk - in' in your sleep.___

Verse 2:
Maybe I'm being foolish
'Cause I haven't heard you mention anybody's name at all
How I wish I could be sure it's me that turns you on
Each time you close your eyes.

She Believes In Me

Words & Music by Steve Gibb

© Copyright 1978 Angel Wing Music Company, USA.
Universal Music Publishing Limited.
All rights in Germany administered by Universal Music Publ. GmbH.
All Rights Reserved. International Copyright Secured.

While she lays sleep-ing,___ I stay out late at night_ and play my songs,___ and some-times all the nights_ can be so long, and it's good when I fin-'ly make it home all a-lone. While she lays dream-ing___ I try to get_ un-dressed with-out the lights,___ then qui-et-ly___ she says,_ "How was your night?" And I come to her___ and say___ it was all right, and I

hold her tight._ And she be - lieves in me,

I'll nev - er know just what she sees_____ in me.___

I told her some - day____ if she was my girl____ I could

change the world___ with my lit - tle songs,__ I was

wrong. But she has faith_____ in me,___

and so I go on try - ing faith - ful - ly,___

and who knows, may - be___ on some spe - cial night___ if my

song is right I will find___ a way,___

find a way. While she lays wait - ing___ I

stum - ble to the kit - chen___ for a bite.___ Then I

see my old gui - tar in___ the night, just

wait - ing for me like___ a se - cret friend, and there's

218

no end. While she lays cry-ing, I fum-ble with a me - lo - dy or___

two, then I'm torn be-tween the things that I should

do. Then she says to wake her up___ when I am

through, God, her love is true.___ And she be-

God, her love is true.___ And she be-

D.S. al Coda

Coda

while she waits,

while___ she waits for me.

He Stopped Loving Her Today

Words & Music by Bobby Braddock & Curly Putman

Very slow

1. He said "I'll love you 'til I die."

(Verses 2-5. see block lyrics)

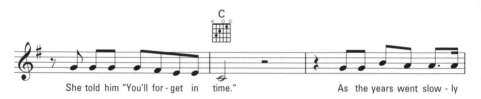

She told him "You'll for-get in time."   As the years went slow-ly

by,   she still preyed up-on his mind.

1-3.   **4, 5.**

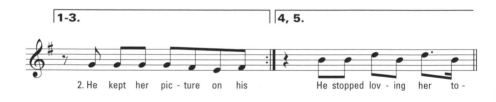

2. He kept her pic-ture on his   He stopped lov-ing her to-

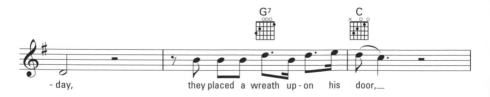

- day,   they placed a wreath up-on his door,___

and soon they'll car - ry him a - way,___

He stopped lov - ing her to - day.___

He stopped lov - ing her to - day.___

Verse 2:
He kept her picture on his wall
Went half crazy now and then
But he still loved her through it all
Hoping she'd come back again.

Verse 3:
He kept some letters by his bed
Dated 1962
He had underlined in red
Every single "I love you."

Verse 4:
I went to see him just today
Oh, but I didn't see no tears
All dressed up to go away
First time I'd seen him smile in years.

Verse 5:
(Spoken)
You know, she came to see him one last time
We all wondered if she would
And it kept running through my mind
This time he's over her for good.

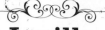

Lucille

Words & Music by Roger Bowling & Hal Bynum

Moderately

1. In a bar in To-le-do, a-cross from the de-pot, on a
(Verses 2 & 3 see block lyrics)

bar stool she took off her ring. I

thought I'd get clos-er, so I walked on ov-er, I

sat down and asked her her name. When the

drinks fin-al-ly hit her she said "I'm no quit-ter, but I

fin-al-ly quit liv-ing on dreams, I'm

222

hun - gry for laugh - ter, and here ev - er af - ter, I'm

1.

af - ter what - ev - er the oth - er life brings."

2, 3.

2. In the wo - man and said: "You picked a

Chorus

fine time to leave me Lu - cille, with

four hun - gry child - ren and a crop in the field.

I've had some bad times, lived through some sad times, but

223

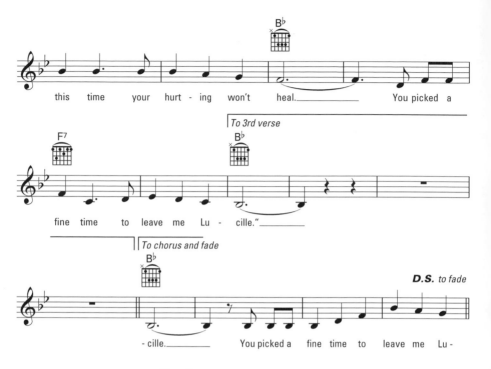

this time your hurt-ing won't heal._____ You picked a

To 3rd verse

fine time to leave me Lu - cille."_____

To chorus and fade

D.S. to fade

- cille._____ You picked a fine time to leave me Lu -

Verse 2:
In the mirror I saw him and I closely watched him
I thought how he looked out of place
He came to the woman who sat there beside me
He had a strange look on his face
The big hands were calloused
He looked like a mountain
For a minute I thought I was dead
But he started shaking
His big heart was breaking
He turned to the woman and said…

Verse 3:
After he left us I ordered more whisky
I thought how she'd made him look small
From the lights of the bar-room
To a rented hotel room
We walked without talking at all
She was a beauty
But when she came to me
She must have thought I'd lost my mind
I couldn't hold her
'Cause the words that he told her
Kept coming back time after time.

The Devil Went Down To Georgia

Words & Music by Charlie Daniels, Fred Edwards,
Jim Marshall, Charlie Hayward, Tom Crain & William Di Gregorio

Lively

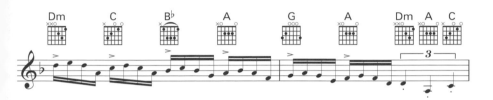

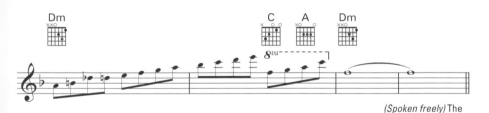

(Spoken freely) The

devil went down to Georgia he was   lookin' for a soul to steal, he was in a
guess you didn't know it but I'm a   fiddle player too,   and

bind 'cause he was behind,   he was   willing to make a deal. When he
if you'd care to take a dare I'll   make a bet with you. Now

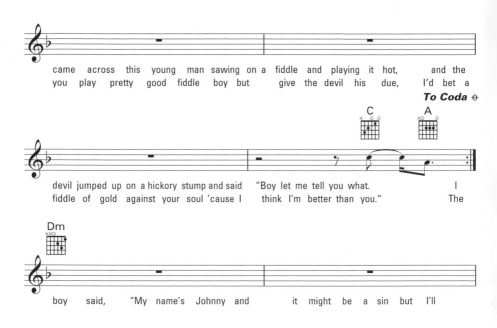

came across this young man sawing on a fiddle and playing it hot,   and the
you play pretty good fiddle boy but   give the devil his due,   I'd bet a

To Coda ⊕

C   A

devil jumped up on a hickory stump and said   "Boy let me tell you what.   I
fiddle of gold against your soul 'cause I   think I'm better than you."   The

Dm

boy said,   "My name's Johnny and   it might be a sin but I'll

take your bet and you're gonna regret 'cause I'm the best there's ever been."

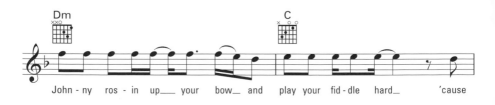

Dm   C

John - ny ros - in up__ your bow__ and   play your fid - dle hard__   'cause

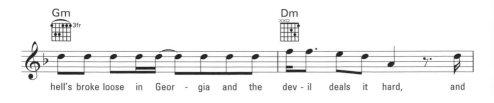

Gm   Dm

hell's broke loose in Geor - gia and the   dev - il deals it hard,   and

226

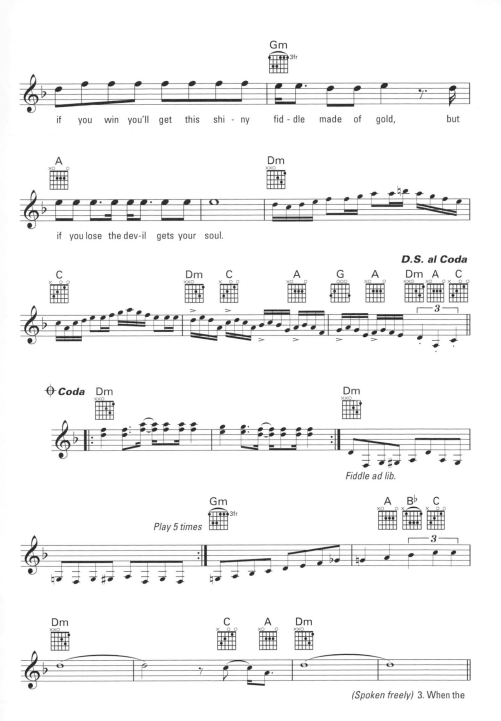

if you win you'll get this shi - ny fid - dle made of gold, but

if you lose the dev-il gets your soul.

D.S. al Coda

Coda

Fiddle ad lib.

Play 5 times

(Spoken freely) 3. When the

227

devil finished Johnny said, "You're pretty good old son, but

sit down in that chair right there and let me show you how it's done."

𝄋𝄋

D

fiddle tacet   fiddle ad lib.
Fire on the moun-tain run___ boys run,___   the

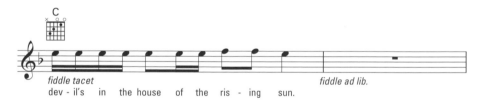

C

fiddle tacet   fiddle ad lib.
dev-il's in the house of the ris - ing sun.

D

fiddle tacet   fiddle ad lib.
Chick-en in the bread pan pick-ing out dough.

C

fiddle tacet   fiddle ad lib.
Gran-ny does your dog bite? No child no.

(Spoken freely) The

The devil bowed his head because he   knew that he'd been beat and he
said "Devil just come on back if you   ever want to try again and I'll

D.S.S. al Fine

laid that golden fiddle on the ground   at Johnny's feet.   Johnny
tell you what, you son of a bitch,   I'm the best there's ever been." He played

Verse 2:
The devil opened up his case
And he said "I'll start this show"
And fire blew from his fingertips as he rosined up his bow
And he pulled the bow across the strings
And it made an evil hiss
Then as a band of demons joined in and it sounded something like this.

Absorbed into the mainstream

Now getting increasingly absorbed into the mainstream, 80s country hits included a Bee Gees composition ('Islands In The Stream') Julie Gold's folksy and quasi-religious 'From A Distance' (popularised by Nanci Griffith and later recorded by Cliff Richard) and the first country No. 1 for Garth Brooks, a man who would go on to employ staggering levels of stagecraft and become a multi-millionaire country superstar. While Brooks smashed guitars and hovered over the stage, Keith Whitley ('When You Say Nothing At All' later covered by Alison Krauss) and Steve Earle, pictured below ('Copperhead Road') were keeping it real.

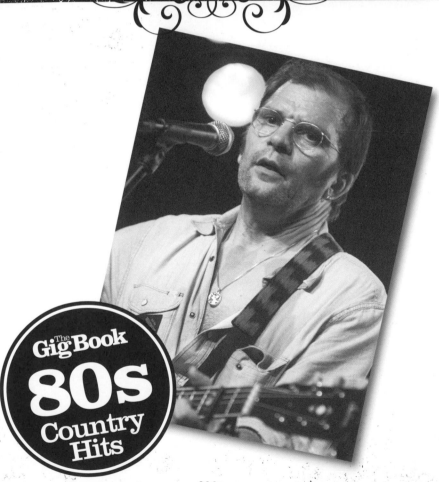

The Gig Book
80s Country Hits

Islands In The Stream

Words & Music by Barry Gibb, Maurice Gibb & Robin Gibb

Slow rock

1. Ba - by when I met you there was peace un - known,　I set out to get you with a
(Verse 2 see block lyrics)

fine tooth comb. I was soft in - side___ there___ was some - thing go - in' on.___

You do some - thing to me that I

can't ex - plain,　hold me clos - er and I feel no pain, ev - 'ry

beat of my heart___ we___ got some - thing go - in' on.___

Ten - der love is blind,　it re - quires___ a de - di - ca - tion.

All this love— we feel needs no con-ver-sa-tion we ride it to-geth-er ah-

-ah,___ mak-in' love___ with each oth-er ah - ah.___ Is-lands in

the stream, that is what we are, no-one in be-tween, how can we

be wrong, sail a-way with me to an-oth-er world, and we re-

-ly on each oth-er ah - ah,___ from one lov - er to an-oth-er ah-

1.

- ah.___

2.

- ah.___

Is-lands in the stream, that is what we are, no-one in be-tween, how can we be wrong sail a-way with me to an-oth-er world and we re-ly on each oth-er ha-hah_____ from one lov-

Repeat and fade

-er to an-oth-er ha-hah._____ Is-lands in

Verse 2:
I can't live without you if the love was gone
Everything is nothing if you got no-one
And you did walk in the night
Slowly losin' sight of the real thing.

But that won't happen to us and we got no doubt
So deep in love and we got no way out
And the message is clear,
This could be the year for the real thing.

No more will you cry, baby I will hurt you never
We start and end as one in love forever
We can ride it together ah-ah
Makin' love with each other ah-ah.

All My Ex's Live In Texas

Words & Music by Lyndia J. Shafer & Sanger D. Shafer

Al - li - son___ in Gal - ves - ton___ some-how lost her san - i - - ty. And Dim - ples who now lives in Tem-ple's got the law look - in'___ for me. light. Some folks think I hide, it's been ru-moured that I died. but I'm a - live and well in Ten - nes - see.___

Verse 2:
I remember that old Brazos River where I learned to swim
But it brings to mind another time where I wore my welcome thin
By transcendental meditation, I go there each night
But I always come back to myself long before daylight.

From A Distance

Words & Music by Julie Gold

Moderately

From a dis-tance the world_ looks blue and green,_ and the
snow - capped_ moun-tains so white. From a dis-tance the oc - ean
meets the stream_ and the ea - gle takes_ to flight. From_ a
dis-tance there_ is har-mo-ny and it e-choes through_ the land._
It's the voice of___ hope,_ it's the voice of___ peace, it's the
voice of___ ev - 'ry - one. From a

dis-tance we all___ have e - nough,__ and no one is_____ in

need. There are no guns, no bombs_ and no_____ dis - ease,_ no

hun - gry mouths___ to feed. For_ a mo-ment we must be

in - stru-ments march-ing in a com-mon band.___ Play-ing

songs of___ hope,_ play-ing songs of___ peace,_ they're the songs of___ ev - 'ry -

- one. God___ is watch - ing us,_____ God___ is

watch-ing us,___ God_ is watch-ing us___ from a dis - tance.___

From a dis-tance you look_ like my friend,_ ev-en though we_ are_ at war. From a dis-tance I_ can't com - pre-hend_ what all this war_ is for. What we need is love_ and har-mo-ny,_ let it e-cho through_ the land._ It's the hope of_ hopes,_ it's the

love of____ loves,_ it's the heart_ of ev - 'ry - one. It's the

hope of____ hopes, it's the love of____ loves,____ it's the

song_ of____ ev - 'ry - one. Sing out

songs of____ hope,____ sing out songs of free - dom, sing out

songs of love,_____ sing out songs of____ peace,_ sing out

songs of jus - tice,____ sing out songs of har - mo - ny,____ sing out

songs of love,____ sing out ev - 'ry - one, sing out.

Alison Krauss

When You Say Nothing At All

Words & Music by Don Schlitz & Paul Overstreet

1. It's a-maz-ing how you___ can speak right___ to my heart,
(Verse 2 see block lyrics)

with-out say-ing a word,___

___ you can light up the dark.___

Try as I may___ I could nev-er ex-plain___

what I hear___ when you don't___ say a thing.___ The

smile on your face___ lets me know___ that you need___ me, there's a

truth in your eyes___ say - ing you'll___ nev - er leave___ me.   A

touch of your hand___ says you'll catch___ me if ev - er I fall.___

___ Now you say it best___

when you say no - thing at all.___

1. **2.**

___ The

smile on your face___ lets me know___ that you need___ me, there's a

242

Verse 2:
All day long I can hear people talking out loud
But when you hold me near, you drown out the crowd
Old Mister Webster could never define
What's being said between your heart and mine.

Copperhead Road

Words & Music by Steve Earle

Moderately

1. Well my name's John Lee Pet - ti - more,

(Verses 2 & 3 see block lyrics)

same as my Dad - dy and his Dad - dy be - fore.

You hard - ly ev - er saw Gran - dad - dy down here,

he on - ly came to town a - bout twice a year.

He'd buy a hun - dred pounds of yeast and some cop - per line,

ev - 'ry - bo - dy knew that he made moon - shine.

Now the rev-en-ue man want-ed Gran-dad-dy bad,

head-ed up the hol-ler with ev - 'ry-thing he had. 'Fore my time but I've_ been told_

nev - er came back from Cop - per-head Road.___

2. Now

(Instrumental)

D.S. al Coda

3. I vol-un-

245

Cop-per-head

Road___   Cop-per-head   Road.___

Verse 2:
Now Daddy ran the whiskey in a big black Dodge
Bought it at an auction at the Mason's Lodge
Johnson County Sheriff painted on the side
Just shot a coat of primer then he looked inside
Well him and my uncle tore that engine down
I still remember that rumblin' sound
Well the sheriff came around in the middle of the night
Heard mama cryin', knew something wasn't right
He was headed down to Knoxville with the weekly load
You could smell the whiskey burnin' down Copperhead Road.

Verse 3:
I volunteered for the Army on my birthday
They draft the white trash first, 'round here anyway
I done two tours of duty in Vietnam
And I came home with a brand new plan
I take the seed from Colombia and Mexico
I plant it up the holler down Copperhead Road
Well the D.E.A.'s got a chopper in the air
I wake up screaming like I'm back over there
I learned a thing or two from ol' Charlie don't you know
You better stay away from Copperhead Road.

If Tomorrow Never Comes

Words & Music by Garth Brooks & Kent Blazy

Slowly

1. Some-times late at night,___
(Verse 2 see block lyrics)

I lie a - wake___ and watch___ her sleep - ing.___ She's

lost in peace-ful dreams,___ so I turn off the lights___ and lay there in the dark.___

___ And the thought cross-es my mind,

if I nev-er wake up in the morn - ing,___

would she ev - er doubt___ the way___ I feel a - bout her in___ my

247

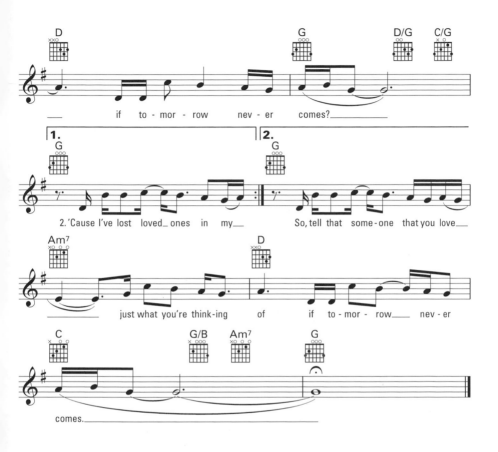

if to - mor - row nev - er comes?

1.
2. 'Cause I've lost loved— ones in my—

2.
So, tell that some - one that you love—

_____ just what you're think-ing of if to - mor - row___ nev - er

comes.___

Verse 2:
'Cause I've lost loved ones in my life
Who never knew how much I loved them
Now I live with the regret
That my true feelings for them never were revealed
So I made a promise to myself
To say each day how much she means to me
And avoid that circumstance
Where there's no second chance to tell her how I feel.
'Cause if tomorrow...

Women in country

became something of a 90s theme. Mother and daughter act The Judds might have seemed an unlikely pairing but they were pure country and their hit 'Love Can Build A Bridge' profited from a more universal sentiment than some of their more down-home material like 'John Deere Tractor'. Mary Chapin Carpenter brought wit and intelligence to her songs—none more so than 'He Thinks He'll Keep Her' while The Dixie Chicks exhibited sassy professionalism from the start long before their withering comment about George Bush (made at a 2003 performance at The Shepherds Bush Empire in London) affected their career back home. Another woman, Shania Twain, (born Eileen Edwards in Ontario) threatened to outdo Garth Brooks with an epic career launched by her 'Come On Over' album that spawned three singles, including the award-winning 'You're Still The One'. For the men multi-instrumentalist and neo-traditional country singer Vince Gill (above) also peaked in the 90s; the man who once turned down the chance to join Dire Straits would host the Country Music Awards ceremony throughout the decade and never brought anything less than a classic country sensibility to any song he performed.

The Dixie Chicks

Love Can Build A Bridge

Words & Music by John Jarvis, Paul Overstreet & Naomi Judd

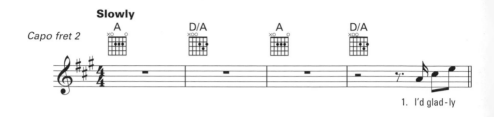

1. I'd glad-ly

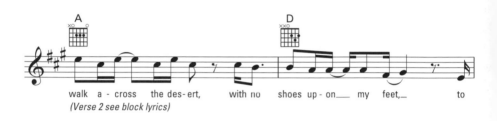

walk a-cross the des-ert, with no shoes up-on__ my feet,__ to
(Verse 2 see block lyrics)

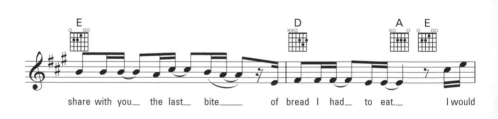

share with you__ the last__ bite_____ of bread I had__ to eat.__ I would

swim out__ to save you in your sea of bro-ken dreams,_____ but

all your hopes are sink - in', let me show you what love means.

Love can build a bridge, be - tween your heart and

mine.___ Love can build a___ bridge, don't you think it's time,___

1.
___ don't you think_ it's time.___

2.
2. I would (Instrumental)

253

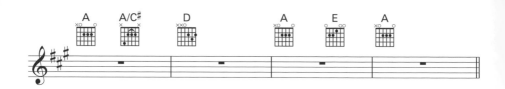

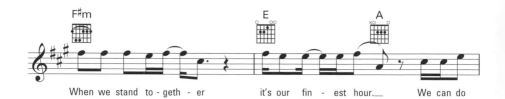

When we stand to-geth-er it's our fin-est hour.__ We can do

a-ny-thing, (a-ny-thing,) a-ny-thing, (a-ny-thing.) Keep be-liev-ing in the pow-

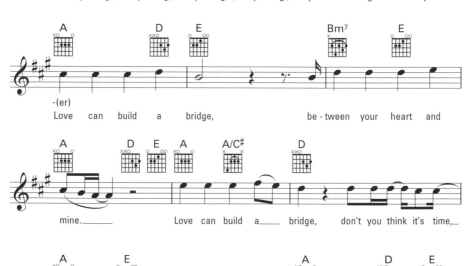

-(er)
Love can build a bridge, be-tween your heart and

mine._____ Love can build a__ bridge, don't you think it's time,__

__ don't you think__ it's time.__

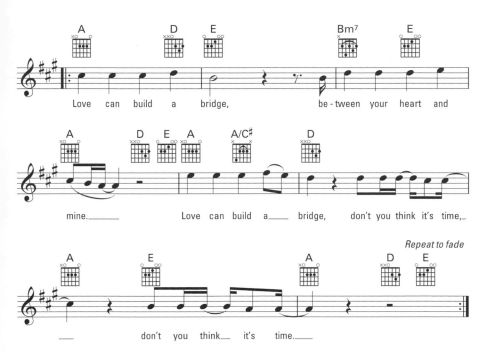

Love can build a bridge, be-tween your heart and mine._____ Love can build a_____ bridge, don't you think it's time,__

Repeat to fade

__ don't you think__ it's time.__

Verse 2:
I would whisper love so loudly
Ev'ry heart would understand
That love and only love
Can join the tribes of man
I would give my heart's desire
So that you might see
The first step is to realise
That it all begins with you and me.

He Thinks He'll Keep Her

Words & Music by Don Schlitz & Mary Chapin Carpenter

Brightly

1. She makes his cof - fee, she makes_ his

(Verses 2 & 3 see block lyrics)

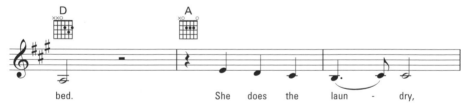

bed. She does the laun - dry,

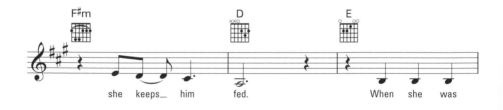

she keeps_ him fed. When she was

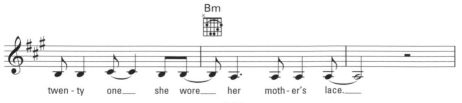

twen - ty one_ she wore_ her moth - er's lace._

you change your mind.___ He thinks he'll keep___ her.

D.S. al Coda I
no repeat

For fif - teen years__ she had a job, and not__

___ one raise in pay. Now she's in the typ -

D.S.S. al Coda II

- ing pool__ at__ min - i - mum wage.__

258

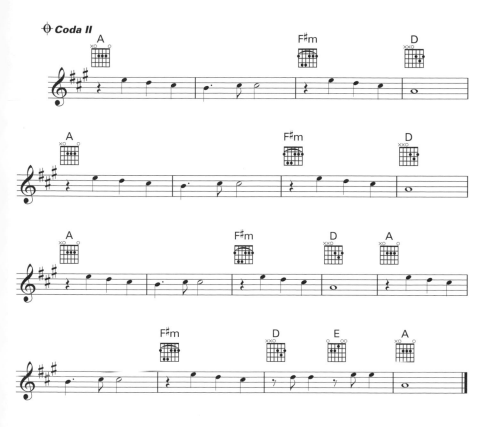

Verse 2:
She does the car-pool, she P.T.A's
Doctors and dentists, she tries all day
When she was twenty-nine she delivered number three
And every Christmas card showed a perfect family.

Verse 3:
She packs his suitcase, she sits and waits
With no expression upon her face
When she was thirty-six she met him at the door
She said I'm sorry, I don't love you anymore.

Pretty Little Adriana

Words & Music by Vince Gill

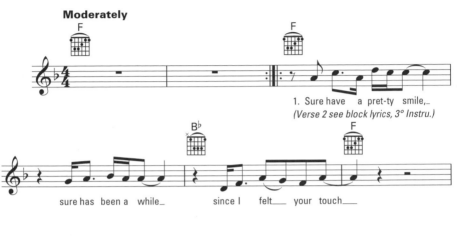

Moderately

1. Sure have a pret-ty smile,_
(Verse 2 see block lyrics, 3° Instru.)

sure has been a while_ since I felt_ your touch___

you've got_ the sweet-est_ way, I think a-bout you ev-'ry day.

I miss you_ so much. Oh_ my pret-ty lit - tle A - dri - a -

- na are you lone - some___ to night?_ Oh_ my

pret - ty lit - tle A - dri - a - na I'll

260

(Vocal ad lib. on repeat)

Verse 2:
So soft and innocent
Sweetest night I ever spent
Was being held in your embrace
You're such a gentle soul
It's killing me to know
When will I see your face?

You're Still The One

Words & Music by Shania Twain & R.J. Lange

Moderately

Capo fret 1

1. Looks like we made it,____ look how far__ we've come my ba - by,
(Verse 2 see block lyrics)

we might have took the long__ way,__ we knew we'd get__there some - day.__

They said, I bet, they'll nev - er make__ it, but just

look at__ us hold - ing__ on we're still to - geth -

- er still go - ing__ strong.____ (Still the one.)

life.   (Still the one.)   You're still the one that   I____   love,____

the on-ly one I dream of,____   you're still the one I kiss__ good - night.

I'm so glad we made   it,   look how far___ we've come my ba - by.

Verse 2:
Ain't nothing better
We beat the odds together
I'm glad we didn't listen
Look at what we would we missing.

There's Your Trouble

Words & Music by Tia Sillers & Mark Selby

Brightly

1. It should have been diff-'rent but it_____ was-n't diff-'rent was it,
(Verse 2 see block lyrics)

same old sto-ry and Dear_____ John, and so long_____

should have fit like a glove,_____ it should have fit like a ring,_____

_____ like a dia-mond ring,_____ to-ken of a true love.

Should have all worked out_____ but it did-n't, she should be here now_

A   **D**   **A/C#**   **Bm7**   **A**

___ but she is - n't.   There's your trou - ble, there's___ you trou - ble,___ keep

G   **D/F#**   **Em**   **A**   **D**   **A/C#**

see - ing dou - ble with a___ wrong___ one___ and you can   see   I love you, you can't___

Bm7   **A**   **G**   **D/F#**   **Em**   **A**

─ see   she does - n't but you   just   keep a hold - in' on.___   There's your

1.
D   **A/C#**   **Bm7**   **A**   **G**   **D/F#**   **Em**   **A**

trou - ble.

2.
D   **A/C#**   **Bm7**   **A**   **G**   **D/F#**   **Em**   **A**

trou - ble.   *(Instrumental)*

D   **A/C#**   **Bm7**   **A**   **G**   **D/F#**   **Em**   **A**

G   **D**   **G**

Should have all worked out___ but it did - n't,   she should be here   now___

266

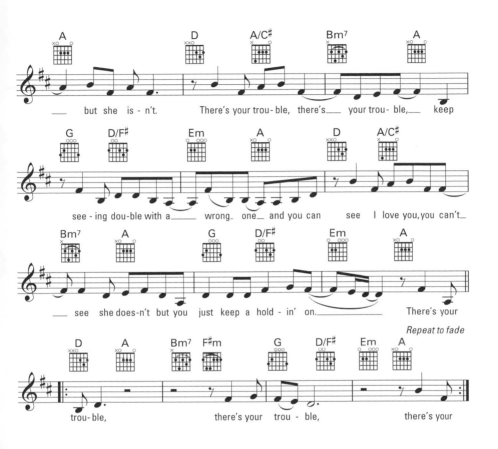

but she is-n't. There's your trou-ble, there's your trou-ble, keep

see-ing dou-ble with a wrong one and you can see I love you, you can't

see she does-n't but you just keep a hold-in' on. There's your

Repeat to fade

trou-ble, there's your trou-ble, there's your

Verse 2:
So now you're thinkin' 'bout all you're missing
How deep you're sinkin' around
And round and dragging down
Why don't you cash in your chips
Why don't you call it a loss
Not such a big loss
Chalk it up, better luck.

267

Amazed

Words & Music by Marv Green, Aimee Mayo & Chris Lindsey

1. Ev-'ry time our eyes meet, this feel-in' in-side me,
(Verse 2 see block lyrics)
is al-most more_ than I_ can take._

Ba-by when you touch me, I can feel how much you love me,

Verse 2:
The smell of your skin, the taste of your kiss
The way you whisper in the dark
You hair all around me, baby you surround me
Touch every place in my heart.
Oh it feels like the first time every time
I wanna spend the whole night in your arms.

3 4 5 6 7 8 9

Garth Brooks